Cambridge

M000287679

Elements in the Philosophy of Physics
edited by
James Owen Weatherall
University of California, Irvine

PHYSICS AND COMPUTATION

Armond Duwell
University of Montana

CAMBRIDGE
UNIVERSITY PRESS

CAMBRIDGE
UNIVERSITY PRESS

University Printing House, Cambridge CB2 8BS, United Kingdom

One Liberty Plaza, 20th Floor, New York, NY 10006, USA

477 Williamstown Road, Port Melbourne, VIC 3207, Australia

314–321, 3rd Floor, Plot 3, Splendor Forum, Jasola District Centre,
New Delhi – 110025, India

103 Penang Road, #05–06/07, Visioncrest Commercial, Singapore 238467

Cambridge University Press is part of the University of Cambridge.

It furthers the University's mission by disseminating knowledge in the pursuit of
education, learning, and research at the highest international levels of excellence.

www.cambridge.org
Information on this title: www.cambridge.org/9781009108553
DOI: 10.1017/9781009104975

First published 2021

A catalogue record for this publication is available from the British Library.

ISBN 978-1-009-10855-3 Paperback

ISSN 2632-413X (online)
ISSN 2632-4121 (print)

Physics and Computation

Elements in the Philosophy of Physics

DOI: 10.1017/9781009104975
First published online: August 2021

Armond Duwell
University of Montana

Author for correspondence: Armond Duwell, armond.duwell@umontana.edu

Abstract: This Element has three main aims. First, it aims to help the reader understand the concept of computation that Turing developed, his corresponding results, and what those results indicate about the limits of computational possibility. Second, it aims to bring the reader up to speed on analyses of computation in physical systems that provide the most general characterizations of what it takes for a physical system to be a computational system. Third, it aims to introduce the reader to some different kinds of quantum computers, describe quantum speedup, and present some explanation sketches of quantum speedup. If successful, this Element will equip the reader with a basic knowledge necessary for pursuing these topics in more detail.

Keywords: quantum computation, quantum speedup, physical Church–Turing thesis, account of computation, quantum computers

ISBNs: 9781009108553 (PB), 9781009104975 (OC)
ISSNs: 2632-413X (online), 2632-4121 (print)

Contents

1 Introduction

Providing a comprehensive introduction to issues in physics and computation within 30,000 words is quite a challenge. Without further ado, here is what to expect. In Section 2, I introduce the reader to Turing's work on the concept of computation, focusing on his 1936 paper. In Section 3, I present the Church–Turing thesis and its ramifications for physical limits on computational possibilities. In Section 4, I present the problem of how to characterize computation in physical systems and some of the accounts that attempt to address it. In Section 5, I introduce the reader to three different types of quantum computers. Finally in Section 6, I explore proposed explanations of quantum speedup.[1] My hope is that by the end of the Element the reader will be equipped with the resources to further pursue investigations into the relation between physics and computation in any of the three different areas articulated above: the limits of computational possibility, accounts of computation in physical systems, or investigations into quantum speedup. That said, this Element isn't merely introductory. New arguments and novel criticisms of different views are distributed throughout.

2 Turing's 1936 Paper

In this section I will briefly present some of the ideas and results from Turing's landmark (1936) paper "On computable numbers, with an application to the Entscheidungsproblem." This is without a doubt one of the great papers of the twentieth century, widely cited and widely misunderstood. I want to inoculate the reader from at least a few misunderstandings by discussing some key points. Most importantly, I will emphasize that, when Turing uses the term "computer," he means "a human performing computations," which is very different from what we now mean by "computer." This fundamental fact is often overlooked and is a key source of confusion that infects discussions of computation. Setting the historical stage properly and explaining Turing (1936) in detail are not among the goals here. For that, I would refer the reader to Copeland (2004). Instead, I want to give the reader the bare-bones understanding of Turing (1936) to serve as a springboard for discussing physics and computation quite generally.

---

[1] In an Element like this, one might expect to find a discussion on Landauer's principle, which states that erasure of n bits of information always incurs a cost of $k \ln n$ in thermodynamic entropy. Unfortunately, there is no space for a discussion of the principle in this Element. See O. Maroney (2009) for an introduction to the issues associated with Landauer's principle.

2.1 Formal Representation of Human Computers

Turing, on the first page of his paper (1936), writes

> We have said that the computable numbers are those whose decimals are
> calculable by finite means. This requires rather more explicit definition. [...]
> For the present I shall only say that the justification lies in the fact that the
> *human* [emphasis added] memory is necessarily limited.

Front and center, it is obvious that in an attempt to characterize the computable numbers, Turing's intent is to characterize the class of numbers whose
decimal expansion could be provided by a human. To do so, Turing provides a mathematical representation of what he views as the essential features
of humans that enable and limit human computational abilities. Turing then
uses this mathematical representation of humans to indicate what the class of
computable numbers is.

Turing's mathematical representation of what is essential to human computing defines what a Turing machine is. A Turing machine is not an actual
machine, but a mathematical construct like circles or triangles. A Turing
machine consists, in part, of an endless tape partitioned into various cells that
are capable of bearing symbols. A Turing machine is equipped with a read/write
head that is capable of reading symbols from a finite set on the cell in the
tape that it is currently positioned over, writing or erasing symbols, and shift-
ing left or right one cell. A Turing machine also has a finite set of internal
states. Particular Turing machines are characterized by their machine table,
which corresponds to what we would now call a program. The machine table
determines the behavior of the machine. Given an internal state and scanned
symbol, which we refer to jointly as the *configuration* of the machine, the
program indicates whether the read/write tape head should erase or write a
symbol, whether the head should move or not, and finally, what internal state to
update to. Machine tables can be represented as sets of instructions of the form
$\langle q_i, s_i, q_j, s_j, d \rangle$, where $q_{i/j}$ are the current/subsequent internal states, $s_{i/j}$ are
the current/subsequent symbols on the tape, which include the blank symbol,
and $d \in \{-1, 0, 1\}$ indicates how the read/write tape head should move.[2] See
Figure 1.

Turing devotes Section 9 of his paper to arguing that Turing machines capture the essential properties of humans performing computations. He draws
our attention to several important aspects of human computations. First, when
humans perform computations, they typically utilize a spatial medium with
distinguishable locations (e.g. a piece of paper with a grid on it). Turing views

---

[2] This notation is not Turing's, but it has the advantage of being more transparent than Turing's.

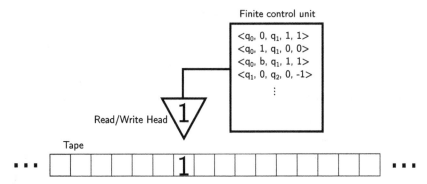

Figure 1 A Turing machine with an unbounded tape divided into cells, a read/write tape head that can move one left or right one cell or stay stationary, and a finite control unit.

the number of dimensions of the medium as being unimportant; hence he represents this aspect of computation with a one-dimensional tape with distinguishable cells. Humans distinguish only a finite number of symbols, hence the limitation of Turing machines to a finite set of symbols. Humans can distinguish only small sequences of symbols at a glance. Turing uses the convincing example of the two (different) numbers 9999999999999999 and 999999999999999 to illustrate the point. Distinguishing these two numbers would involve some sort of procedure. Turing thinks that it is no computational limitation to distinguish only one symbol at a time and use memory to recover the whole number. Hence, the read/write head on a Turing machine reads a single symbol at a time. Humans can change only a single symbol at a time, and so too can the read/write head. Turing portrays humans as having only a finite number of states of mind, hence a finite number of internal states for Turing machines. The state of mind of a human computer and the symbol or symbols in view determine the next state of mind and action on the page in terms of where attention is directed to and what is done to symbols on the page. Similarly, the internal state and scanned symbol determine what a Turing machine does next to update its configuration. Humans utilize a finite set of primitive operations when performing a computation, and computers do too. Those primitive operations involve a change of symbol on the page with a possible change of mind, or a possible change of observed squares, together with a change of mind. Primitive operations of a Turing machine are similar. They involve a change of symbol on the tape along with a possible change of internal state, or a change of scanned tape cell together with a change in internal state. Clearly Turing aimed to represent the essential features of human computers mathematically with his machines.[3]

---

[3] Turing's portrayal of human computational abilities involves no elements of chance, insight, intuition, or ingenuity, and his results should be understood accordingly.

2.2 The Results

What are the computable numbers? Computable numbers are any infinite decimal that can be generated by a Turing machine and may or may not be prefaced by an integer.[4] So, Turing machines that halt (i.e. stop after some finite number of basic operations) do not correspond to computable numbers, as defined by Turing. Copeland (2004, 33) notes that this use of "computable number" might seem too restrictive. Modern writers consider finite sequences generated by Turing machines as corresponding to computable numbers as well.

In addition to developing a representation of human computers and providing a definition of computable numbers, Turing developed the notion of a *universal* Turing machine. A universal Turing machine was a machine that could take as an input on a tape a description of a particular Turing machine and then emulate its output behavior. As remarked above, Turing machines can be described by their machine tables. These tables are just lists of instructions. Turing came up with an encoding scheme so that each distinct list of instructions was associated with a distinct number, called the *description number of the machine*. From that number one can produce the the *standard description* of a Turing machine and use it as input to a universal machine, and it will produce the output of the machine associated with the standard description. By showing how to assign description numbers to Turing machines, Turing demonstrated that the class of computable numbers was enumerable.

Turing also argued that the Entscheidungproblem is not solvable. The Entscheidungsproblem was articulated in Hilbert and Ackermann's (1928) *Grundzüge der theoretischen Logik*. The problem, as described therein, is to determine whether or not a given formula of the predicate calculus is universally valid, or whether those formulas are deducible from the axiom system of the predicate calculus, or whether a sentence of the predicate calculus is satisfiable. These are three equivalent ways of stating the problem (Davies, 2013). The problem was understood as inquiring into *our* limitations. Turing's proof of the undecidability of the Entscheidungsproblem proceeded by showing the following (Del Mol, 2019, Sec 2.4.2):

1. how, for each Turing machine *T*, it is possible to construct a corresponding formula **T** in first-order logic and
2. if there is a general method for determining whether **T** is provable, then there is a general method for proving that *T* will ever print 0.

---

[4] Note that the concept of a computable number is still highly idealized. Computable numbers cannot actually be computed!

Turing proved that there was no general method for proving that T will ever print 0, hence the Enscheidungsproblem is undecidable.[5]

In an appendix to his paper, Turing showed that the computable numbers coincided with the class of numbers identified by Church (1936) as the "effectively calculable" numbers.

It is worth emphasizing that our concept of computation arose from discussions in the foundations of mathematics between Church, Kleene, Gödel, and Post, among others. That said, for the purposes of this Element, what concerns us are the possible implications of this work in foundations of mathematics for what is computable, what a computer is, and how to identify what number, function, or other thing a computer is computing.[6] We are interested in computation in physical systems. It is to these topics that we now turn.

3 The Church–Turing Thesis and the Physical Church–Turing Thesis

In this section we explore possible limitations to our computational capacities. Both the Church–Turing Thesis and the physical Church–Turing thesis will be discussed. The Church–Turing thesis is widely misunderstood as making claims about what is computationally possible, but, as will be argued below, it is almost definitional in character. The physical Church–Turing thesis, something completely different, can be very coarsely construed as the claim that the computational power of Turing machines cannot be exceeded.[7] Given what we have learned in Section 2, this would be a remarkable fact, as Turing machines are just formal representations of human computational abilities. Can no physical system do better? Let us investigate.[8]

3.1 The Church–Turing Thesis

As we have seen, Turing set out to describe the class of numbers that are computable by humans. Even so, it is not obvious that the class of numbers that he identified is the right class. The kind of processes that Turing machines represent are those that leave no room for insight, intuition, or ingenuity. Given that humans do have insight, intuition, or ingenuity, it would seem that there

---

[5] For more details about how Turing carried out the proof of the undecidability of the Entscheidungsproblem, see Del Mol (2019).

[6] I am grateful to an anonymous referee for suggesting that this point be emphasized.

[7] See Pitowsky (2007) for a description of how theses about computation change over time.

[8] For a more detailed discussion of these matters, see Copeland (2019) and Piccinini (2015), chapters 15 and 16. Copeland, Shagrir, and Sprevak (2018) also discuss these matters and related ones.

are functions that might be computable by humans that have not been captured by Turing. It is perfectly reasonable if the reader is puzzled.

Puzzlement can be dispelled, in part, by considering a problem that had become pressing in the foundations of mathematics in the 1920s and 1930s: that of defining what an effectively calculable function was, where *effectively calculable* was understood in an informal way. Copeland (2019) provides a useful definition:

> A method, or procedure, *M*, for achieving some desired result is called "effective" (or "systematic" or "mechanical") just in case:
>
> *M* is set out in terms of a finite number of exact instructions (each instruction being expressed by means of a finite number of symbols);
>
> *M* will, if carried out without error, produce the desired result in a finite number of steps;
>
> *M* can (in practice or in principle) be carried out by a human being unaided by any machinery except paper and pencil;
>
> *M* demands no insight, intuition, or ingenuity, on the part of the human being carrying out the method.[9]

An effectively calculable function (or number, or whatever) is one that is calculable by an effective method.[10]

The precision of Copeland's characterization of effective method and corresponding characterization of effectively calculable function should not lead one to believe that the concept was just as clear in the minds of mathematicians and logicians in the 1920s and 1930s, though no doubt something of the sort was present.

Several candidate precisifications for the intuitive concept of effectively calculable function were given in the 1930s. Church (1937) suggested that the class of λ-definable functions was the set of effectively calculable functions. In footnote 3 of that paper, Church notes that work by Kleene, Church, and Rosser shows that the λ-definable functions are also the recursive functions, characterized in Gödel's 1934 lectures at Princeton. It is worth noting that Gödel was at the Institute for Advanced Studies, Church was a professor of mathematics at Princeton, and Kleene and Rosser were his graduate students. The claim that the effectively calculable functions were the λ-definable functions or the recursive functions came to be known as *Church's thesis*.[11]

---

[9] See Piccinini (2015, 247) for an alternative characterization for an effective process.

[10] Copeland (2019) provides a useful example of the connection between computable number and computable function: "For example, the computable number .14159... (formed of the digits following the decimal point in π, 3.1419...) corresponds to the computable function: f(1) = 1, f(2) = 4, f(3) = 1, f(4) = 5, f(6) = 9,...".

[11] Copeland (2019) calls Church's thesis the claim that a function of positive integers is effectively calculable *only if* λ-definable (or, equivalently, recursive), and distinguishes it from the

Turing can be seen as providing a precisification of the concept of effectively calculable function.

It is reasonable to assume that Turing had something like the concept of an effective method in mind when he wrote his 1936 paper. The first line of the paper reads, "The 'computable' numbers may be described briefly as the real numbers whose expressions as a decimal are calculable by finite means." On that page, he writes that the justification for this definition of computable numbers "lies in the fact that human memory is limited." The reference to finite means and human memory on that first page suggests that Turing did have in mind something like an effectively calculable number (or function) as defined above, though he used the phrase "computable function" instead.

Now, back to our puzzle: Why think that Turing had succeeded in identifying the *humanly* computable numbers, functions, and so on when human abilities like insight, intuition, or ingenuity are not taken into account? It was because Turing had in mind the concept of effective method when he considered human computational abilities, and that excluded insight, intuition, or ingenuity. Such a concept had been of increasing importance in the 1920s and early 1930s, in part because of Hilbert's program to put mathematics on solid epistemological footing, and also due to Gödel's incompleteness results.[12]

The reader has likely anticipated what Turing's thesis is, but it does deserve to be explicitly stated. *Turing's thesis* is that a number, function, or anything else is effectively calculable only if computable by a Turing machine. Turing (1937) demonstrated that the class of λ-definable functions was equivalent to the class of functions computable by a Turing machine and that that class of functions was equivalent to the class of recursive functions. So, Church's thesis and Turing's thesis pick out the same class of functions. One rendering of the Church–Turing thesis is that a function is effectively calculable only if Turing computable or λ-definable or recursive. This captures Kleene's intent when he first used the phrase "Church–Turing Thesis" in his 1967 book.

The question of whether the Church–Turing thesis is true naturally arises. The concept of an effectively computable function was imprecise, but shared among those working in foundations of mathematics and logic in the early twentieth century. Whether the thesis is "true" depends on whether Church or Turing provided the appropriate precisification of the concept of an effectively

---

converse of the thesis, that a function of the positive integers is effectively calculable *if* it is λ-definable. He does note that Church himself didn't distinguish between the two.

[12] Sieg (1994) is an excellent resource for understanding why people interested in the foundations of logic and mathematics were concerned about clarifying the concept of an effectively calculable function or the related concept of effective method.

calculable function as it was understood by those employing the concept. On that matter, it seems like the thesis was accepted by those concerned. Church (1937, 43) writes, "It is thus immediately clear that computability, so defined, can be identified with (especially is no less general than) the notion of effectiveness as it appears in certain mathematical problems (various forms of the Entscheidungsproblem, various problems to find complete sets of invariants in topology, group theory, etc., and in general any problem which concerns the discovery of an algorithm)." It is of note, and well known, that Gödel did not accept Church's thesis, but did accept Turing's thesis. What is of significant difference between Church's presentation of his thesis (1936) and Turing's presentation (1936) was that Turing made it transparent how his machines could represent humans using an effective method for calculation of numbers (and functions too). Insofar as Turing machines adequately represented effective methods for the calculation of numbers, one should be confident that the limitations of the machines would be limitations of effective calculability.[13] So, the Church–Turing thesis does seem to be true, but it is almost trivially so, given that it has an almost definitional status. Further evidence that the thesis is true comes from the fact that alternative representations of effective methods arrive at the same class of functions that Turing and Church arrived at as detailed in Kleene (1953).[14]

Given the above discussion, it should be reasonably clear that the Church–Turing thesis, even if true, is rather limited. It does not imply anything about what computers can do, when "computers" is understood as it is today as "a system that we use to perform computational tasks" rather than how Turing understood the term. Using Turing's version of the thesis, recall that it states that *if* a function is effectively calculable, *then* it is calculable by a Turing machine. In the contrapositive, if a Turing machine cannot compute a function, then it is not effectively calculable. "Effectively calculable" has the essential connection to a human process lacking insight, intuition, or ingenuity. The thesis, if true, circumscribes what is possible *given certain limited means*. There seems to be no prima facie reason for thinking that the Church–Turing thesis, if true, circumscribes what is computationally possible in the contemporary sense. One can reasonably expect that human capabilities extend beyond what Turing machines are capable of because we do have insight, intuition, or ingenuity. Moreover, we could expect that systems characterized by physical processes very different from those a Turing machine has available to it would have

---

[13] Turing also offered another argument in Section 9 of his paper (1936). See Copeland (2019) for a discussion.

[14] Kripke (2013) argues that the Church–Turing thesis does admit proof, and he attempts to provide one. See Copeland (2019) for an overview of Kripke's proof.

different computational abilities. It is also of note that the Church–Turing thesis, even if true, does not provide any indication about what computations can be done efficiently. Recall that computable numbers are computed by Turing machines that never halt! If one wants to be in the business of making claims about what is computationally possible or what is efficiently computable, then one has to go beyond the Church–Turing thesis.[15]

3.2 Beyond the Church–Turing Thesis

Given what the Church–Turing thesis actually claims, it may seem rather underwhelming compared to the grandiose claims that have been made regarding it. That is because many of the claims attributed to the Church–Turing thesis ought to be attributed to a completely different set of theses: the *simulation thesis* and the *maximality thesis*.[16]

Simulation thesis: Turing machines can simulate any physical system to any degree of approximation.[17]

Maximality thesis: All functions that can be generated by machines (working in accordance with a finite program of instructions) are computable by effective methods (Copeland, 2019).

These distinct theses are often combined into what is referred to as the *physical Church–Turing thesis*, which has many nonequivalent formulations. For conceptual clarity, it is useful to distinguish the simulation and maximality theses.

It has been emphasized in Copeland (2002) and Piccinini (2015, Ch. 15) that, when investigating issues relating to the physical Church–Turing thesis, one should distinguish between theses as they apply to physical possibilities broadly or narrowly construed. Construed narrowly, one can consider the truth of the above theses with respect to our best physical theories and conditions present in the actual world. Construed broadly, one can consider the truth of the above theses with respect to our best theories, ignoring actual conditions, or even more broadly constrained only by logical possibility. Let us examine the above theses with such distinctions in mind.[18]

---

[15] See Copeland (2019, sec. 2) for a discussion of the many ways in which the Church–Turing thesis has been misunderstood.

[16] With respect to confusions regarding the Church–Turing thesis, one might also add to the list a claim to the effect that the efficiency of simulations on Turing machines is correlated to the efficiency of other physical processes. Quantum speedup, as discussed in section 6, seems to refute this.

[17] See Copeland (2019) and Pitowsky (2002) for alternative formulations of the simulation thesis.

[18] For an alternative conceptualization of the various issues involved in the physical Church–Turing thesis, see Piccinini (2015, Ch. 15).

3.3 The Simulation Thesis

The simulation thesis claims that Turing machines can simulate any physical system to any degree of approximation. The simulation thesis appears to be straightforwardly false when properly understood. Piccinini (2015) points out that one ought to disallow Turing machines that instantiate input output tables that are programmed directly into a Turing machine from counting as simulating physical systems. This stands to reason, if we want to capture the concept of simulation as it is used in science. Simulations are used in practice to *predict* how systems of interest will behave. If one programs a Turing machine using a lookup table, that means that one needs to have the lookup table in hand prior to programming the Turing machine. To do so, one must already know how the system of interest behaves in every possible case. So, rather than predicting how a system of interest might behave in a particular situation, Turing machines that are programmed with a lookup table are just describing how the system will behave. The simulation thesis, if it is to have any significance, ought to make claims about simulation in practice, else it suffers from triviality. Let us turn to the evidence against the thesis, understood in its nontrivial sense.

The existence of some chaotic systems is devastating to the simulation thesis. Some chaotic systems are such that no matter how precisely we specify initial conditions, there will be a time at which we fail to predict the behavior of the system. Evidence of the existence of such systems does not come only from highly idealized mathematical models. We need only turn our attention to the double pendulum. Shinbrot et al. (1992) take pains to create two identical pendulums that are released in as identical as possible initial conditions, yet the two systems diverge in behavior very quickly. Our theoretical models of such systems predict this behavior as well. If there exist systems that diverge so quickly, the simulation thesis doesn't even get a foot in the door. Even if we knew exactly what the laws of the world are, we don't have the right control to have systems evolve identically. So, even if the laws of physics were computable, we cannot create, much less specify, initial conditions that would allow one to simulate the behavior of some physical systems for any extended length of time.

Advocates of the simulation thesis might retort that this violates the spirit of the simulation thesis. In such cases, it is no fault of Turing machines that they fail to simulate a system. They might think that there is no reason to believe that, *if* we could precisely specify the initial conditions, Turing machines would fail to be able to predict behavior. This would be a significant weakening of the simulation thesis. In any case, it is not a promising response. If the initial conditions are computable in Turing's sense, as discussed in Section 2.2, a Turing machine to generate the initial values would never halt. If one settled for less than a complete specification of initial values, then we expect simulation to fail on the basis of our models of chaotic systems. Furthermore, the computable numbers are countably infinite, yet real numbers are not. For any system whose initial conditions are real valued, there will be initial conditions that are not computable, hence predictions about that future behavior of the system are uncomputable in principle.

An advocate of the simulation thesis might point out that one will never have the control to place a system in any such state and make an appeal to a class of *effectively computable* reals (described below) that should be sufficient to describe our experimental capabilities. Such a response is not particularly convincing because it takes us away from entertaining counterfactual possibilities that might save a simulation thesis less ambitious than the one articulated above and back to real-world cases that provide strong evidence against the thesis in the first place. In case anyone would want to pursue it nonetheless, one runs into considerable theoretical difficulties.

To discuss these difficulties, we need to define *effectively computable* functions. As Earman (1986) remarks, the path to effective computability is to "move along the well-charted path from the integers through the rationals to the reals, effectivising definitions as we go" (116). Grzegorczyk (1957) provides the definitions. I follow Pour-El and Richards (1981) closely in laying out the requisite definitions, making minor departures in terminology to bring it in line with what the reader is familiar with from this Element so far.

EFFECTIVELY COMPUTABLE NUMBERS AND FUNCTIONS

A sequence $\{r_n\}$ of rational numbers is effectively computable if there exist Turing computable functions a, b, and c from $\mathbb{N} \to \mathbb{N}$ such that

$$r_n = (-1)^{c(n)} \frac{a(n)}{b(n)}.$$

A real number x is effectively computable if there exists a computable sequence of rationals $\{r_n\}$ that converges effectively to x. This is so when there exists a computable function of the natural numbers, $e(n)$, so that whenever $k \geq e(n)$, then $|x - r_k| \leq 10^{-n}$. We can use $e(n)$ to generate a computable subsequence $\{r'_n\} = \{r_{e(n)}\}$ so that $|x - r'_n| \leq 10^{-n}$. A sequence of real numbers $\{x_k\}$ is effectively computable if there is a computable double sequence of rationals $\{r_{nk}\}$ such that $|x_k - r_{kn}| \leq 10^{-n}$ for all k and n.

A function f of the reals is effectively computable if

- f is *sequentially computable*, that is, for every effectively computable sequence $\{x_k\}$ of points, the sequence of values $\{f(x_k)\}$ is effectively computable; and
- f is *effectively uniformly continuous*, that is, there exists a Turing computable function $d(n)$ such that for all $x, y \in \mathbb{R}$

$$|x - y| \le 1/d(n) \text{ implies } |f(x) - f(y)| \le 10^{-n}.$$

Let us return to the objection that, when evaluating the simulation thesis, we should think of preparing systems only with effectively computable real values instead of actual real values. This too seems to provide no respite for an advocate of the simulation thesis. The difficulty that one runs into is a result in Pour-El and Richards (1981).

Pour-El and Richards consider the wave equation

$$\frac{\partial^2 u}{dx^2} + \frac{\partial^2 u}{dy^2} + \frac{\partial^2 u}{dz^2} - \frac{\partial^2 u}{dt^2} = 0 \tag{3.1}$$

with initial conditions

$$u(x, y, z, t) = f(x, y, z),$$
$$\frac{\partial u}{dt}(x, y, z, 0) = 0.$$

They show that there is an effectively computable function $f(x, y, z)$ where the solution $u(x, y, z, t)$ is continuous but not effectively computable, and furthermore, the value $u(0, 0, 0, 1)$ is not an effectively computable real number.

So, an advocate of a weakened simulation thesis still has problems. The function f could represent a physical system, yet a Turing machine could not compute the time evolution of the system, even if we had exquisite control of the initial values of the system. For this reason, and all of those discussed above, the simulation thesis seems quite difficult to save.

A weakened simulation thesis might still be viable: if the initial conditions of a system are well represented by effectively computable numbers (and they need not be), and if we could identify the initial conditions (and we need not be able to), and if, as a contingent feature of our universe, such a system is not well represented by functions like the ones Pour-El and Richards identified for us, then a Turing machine could simulate that system to any degree of accuracy.

Given the list of antecedents, it seems unlikely that the weakened simulation thesis conveys anything of fundamental significance about our world.[19]

3.4 The Maximality Thesis

The maximality thesis claims that the class of calculations that can be done by any machines with a finite set of instructions is equivalent to the class of calculations that can be done by Turing machines. Note that the claim is *restricted* to machines that have finite program instructions and makes *no* claims about what can be done with arbitrary physical systems. Even so, it is prima facie not something that one would expect to be true given how Turing was thinking about computation. Nonetheless, Gandy (1980) presented interesting evidence to the contrary.

Gandy (1980) proved that any physical system satisfying a particular set of constraints can generate the same functions a Turing machine can. Copeland and Shagrir (2007) provide a useful simplification of Gandy's constraints:

Form of Description Any discrete deterministic mechanical device M can be described by $\langle S, F_i \rangle$, where S is a structural class, and F is a transformation from S_i to S_j. Thus, if S_0 is M's initial state, then $F(S_0)$, $F(F(S_0))$,...are its subsequent states.

Limitation of Hierarchy Each state S_i of S can be assembled from parts, which can be assemblages of other parts, and so on, but there is a finite bound on the complexity of this structure.

Unique Reassembly Each state S_i of S is assembled from basic parts (of bounded size) drawn from a reservoir containing a bounded number of types of basic parts.

Local Causation Parts from which $F(x)$ can be reassembled depend only on bounded parts of x.[20]

The first thing to note about Gandy's constraints is that they certainly do not apply to non-discrete or indeterministic devices. So, Gandy's result is certainly *not* that the only functions that are computable (in today's sense of the word) are those identified by Church and Turing. It is nonetheless remarkable that the class of systems identified by Gandy can only generate the same functions that Turing machines can. An additional issue is whether Gandy has properly identified the class of functions that *any* discrete deterministic mechanical device can compute.

---

[19] For a different view of the significance of the Pour-El and Richards result, see Pitowsky (1990).
[20] For a more detailed presentation of Gandy's constraints, see Gandy (1980) or Sieg (2002b).

This issue depends on whether there are good reasons for thinking that Gandy's constraints coincide with what we want to call a discrete deterministic mechanical device. The easiest issue is to decide what one wants to call a machine. I am going to assume that machines are mechanisms. A mechanism is characterized by a set of components. Each of the components has a set of capacities, and the capacities of the mechanism are due to the arrangement and capacities of the components. Components themselves can be mechanisms too. Gandy's constraints identify a subclass of mechanisms so characterized in a number of ways. The *Limitation of Hierarchy* is meant to enforce discreteness of machines. The states must in a sense be finitely describable. The contrast class here consists of analog machines whose states are not *precisely* describable by finite means. The other two restrictions are seemingly unproblematic. *Unique Reassembly* requires that there are a bounded number of *types* of components of a machine and these parts are of bounded size. As Sieg (2002a, 400) puts it, "any state of a concrete machine can be built up from (finitely many different types of) off-the-shelf components." *Local Causation* enforces an upper bound on how quickly changes can propagate through a machine's components. Restrictions on propagation are commensurable with what we know from relativity. The *Form of Description* requirement is not so innocent, as described below.

Gandy's requirements for discrete deterministic computing devices appear to be too strong. The following example originates in Pitowsky (1990) and was developed by Malament, Hogarth (1992), and Earman and Norton (1993). Consider two future-directed curves, λ_1 and λ_2. Suppose that λ_2 is traversable by an observer in a finite amount of proper time and intersects point p. Let λ_1 be an endless future-directed curve in the backward light cone of p. Suppose further that an observer traversing λ_1 requires an infinite amount of proper time. Suppose a Turing machine, TM_1, is programmed to check Goldbach's conjecture, whether every even number greater than 2 is the sum of two primes, by checking it for 2, then 4, then 6, ad infinitum. Equip this Turing machine with a signaling device that signals if and only if an exception is found. Send this Turing machine with signaling device along λ_1 while another Turing machine, TM_2, traverses λ_2. At p, TM_2 would have received a signal from TM_1 if and only if Goldbach's conjecture were false. So, the pair of Turing machines would have solved an uncomputable problem, hence a Gandy-uncomputable problem. See Figure 2.

Copeland and Shagrir (2007) provide a useful diagnosis of why Gandy's analysis does not apply. *Form of Description* requires that the final state of the computation system be determined by its initial state via $F(S_0)$, $F(F(S_0))$, ... That said, in the case where no exception is found to Goldbach's conjecture,

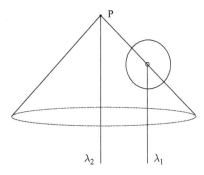

Figure 2 Turing machine TM_1 traverses λ_1, which takes an endless amount of proper time. The circle can represent a region of space-time that "provides" the endless proper time for TM_1. TM_1 checks Goldbach's conjecture and signals only if an exception has been found. Turing TM_2 traverses λ_2. If TM_2 receives a signal, then the conjecture is false; if it doesn't receive a signal, then the conjecture is true. This figure was adapted from Earman and Norton (1993).

there is no final state of TM_1 for the final state of TM_2 to be determined by. So, it appears that Gandy's assumptions are too strong regarding deterministic systems.

In addition to illuminating a problematic assumption made by Gandy in characterizing determinism, the above example undermines the maximality thesis directly. The example appears to indicate that we can transcend the bounds of Turing computability, ironically, using a pair of Turing machines and some interesting space-time structure. It does not show that the maximality thesis is false by appealing to a logically but not physically possible system, as many examples do (see Copeland [2002] for many such examples). Instead, the example is at least potentially physically possible. The hedge in the last statement is due to the fact that while there is no question that the space-time appealed to in the example, known as a Malament-Hogarth space-time, is possible relative to general relativity, there are questions about whether the proposed algorithm will work as advertised. Earman and Norton (1993) provide a careful examination of these issues.

Perhaps the most important problem raised in Earman and Norton (1993) is that the space-time structure in the above example acts as an amplifier for signals propagating from TM_1 to TM_2. If the signal is a photon, it will undergo an indefinite blueshift and hence have indefinite energy. So, the signal will destroy TM_2, and the computation will fail. Andréka, Madarász, Németi, Németi, and Székely (2018) discuss alternative ways to use relativistic space-time structure to solve this problem (among others) and have responded to many objections to relativistic computing. Even so, to date, there are no examples of algorithms that are uncontroversially physically possible to execute that will allow one to transcend the bounds of Turing computability.[21]

3.5 Conclusion

This section has investigated the Church–Turing, simulation, and maximaity theses which are often conflated under the heading of the physical Church–Turing thesis. The Church–Turing thesis delimits what functions can be evaluated by effective methods associated with what humans can do with limited resources and without any appeal to insight, intuition, or ingenuity. Insofar as Turing machines are a good representation of effective methods, then their computational limits should reflect the limits of effective methods. It is obvious that Turing machines are a good representation of effective methods, and furthermore, alternative attempts to represent effective methods result in the same class of functions being identified as effectively computable. So, the evidence for the thesis is quite strong. That said, the limitations of the thesis are apparent. It only tells us what functions can be computed by effective methods, not what might be computed using what might be ironically referred to as "non-effective" methods.

This is where one ought to consider the simulation thesis and the maximality thesis. The simulation thesis claims that a Turing machine can simulate any physical system with arbitrary accuracy. I have argued that the thesis admits of a real world counterexample in the case of the double pendulum. Theoretical considerations also weigh against the simulation thesis. The maximality thesis claims that the class of calculations that can be done by any machines with a finite set of instructions is equivalent to the class of calculations that can be done by Turing machines. This thesis is demonstrably false if we are willing to consider logically, but not physically possible examples. If we are willing to consider only physically possible examples, the evidence is mixed for the maximality thesis. There are cases of initially physically plausible counterexamples to the thesis, but further scrutiny reveals that they are not as plausible as they first appear. It would be a stunning fact if the class of functions computable by humans with finite instructions and pencil and paper would exhaust the universe's computational abilities.

---

[21] See Piccinini (2015, Ch.16) and Andréka et al. (2018) for a more complete discussion of these issues.

An anonymous referee has suggested that the issues could be flipped on their head: we might use the maximality thesis as a guide to physical possibility. This may prove an interesting line of theorizing, but it has a significant limitation. It would provide no explanation for why the maximality thesis might be true; but the truth or falsity of the thesis surely depends on the fundamental physics of our universe.

4 Accounts of Computational Implementation

Turing (1936) was a monumental paper in the history of science. As discussed in Section 2, it defined the computable numbers, developed the concept of a universal programmable computer, and demonstrated that the Entscheidungsproblem had no solution. Nonetheless, Turing certainly did not provide an account of computation in physical systems, though he certainly provided us with a set of insights that have been extremely valuable for developing an account.

An account of computation in physical systems must answer two questions, as characterized in Sprevak (2018, 3):

1. Under which conditions does a physical system implement a computation?
2. Under which conditions does a physical system implement one computation rather than another?

A very natural starting point is to make use of the formalisms that computer scientists use to study computation. Putnam (1988) made use of this idea to develop an initially plausible condition for a system to compute a function. His suggestion was that a system computes a function when there exists a mapping between a particular abstract computational model and a system. By an abstract computational model, I mean those particular models of abstract formalisms that computer scientists typically employ (e.g. particular Turing machines, particular finite state automata, particular circuits). One can associate a state space with each of these particular models. If there exists a mapping between the sequence of states occupied by a computational model in the course of a computation and the sequence of states of a particular system, then that system implements the computation. Following Godfrey-Smith (2009), we call this the simple-mapping account of computation.

Putnam's realization theorem, as Scheutz (1999) calls it, shows us how to cook up a mapping from the state space of an open system to the state space of *any* finite state automaton, a paradigmatic computational model. A similar problem was raised by Searle (1992). He suggested that there will be some pattern of molecular motions or interactions on the wall behind his head that are isomorphic to the formal sequence of states of the WordStar program. The Putnam/Searle problem is that if we only require a physical state-to-computational state correspondence as an account of computational implementation, it leads to pancomputationalism. Not only does everything compute, everything computes every computation, which trivializes computation. The simple mapping account of computation fails *spectacularly*. Furthermore, obvious attempts to save something like the simple mapping account fail. For example, it would seem obvious to require that the mapping have something like a counterfactual element to it so that the computation would be successful for any possible input. Chalmers (1996) shows that this won't save the simple mapping account from triviality either.

The purpose of this section is to introduce the reader to accounts of computation. No attempt is made to provide a comprehensive history of those developments, detailing every alternative and their corresponding strengths and weaknesses. Instead, I aim to equip the reader with a sense of important distinctions and give them a set of reasonable desiderata for evaluating different accounts of computation. I will present the mechanistic account, which largely succeeds at satisfying reasonable desiderata for an account of computation, and an additional recent account, which has garnered a good bit of attention outside of philosophical circles in computer science and physics.

4.1 Desiderata for Accounts of Computation in Physical Systems

All accounts of computation need to solve the Putnam/Searle problem. Doing so is typically not thought to be enough to satisfy our intuitions about what an analysis of computation should do for us. Toward that end, Piccinini (2007) and (2015) have developed a set of desiderata for analyses of computation that have been extremely useful.

4.1.1 Objectivity

An account of computation should make it a matter of fact, rather than a matter of interpretation, about which systems compute and what they compute. Piccinini's motivation for this desideratum is to square accounts of computation with scientific practice. As a matter of fact, scientists use empirical investigation to investigate properties of systems to determine what computational tasks they might contribute to.

This desideratum can be interpreted more or less strongly, leading to two different senses of objectivity.

Let us say that an account of computation satisfies *Strong Objectivity* when it entails that whether a system is computational is completely mind-independent. An account cannot do so if it makes any appeal to minds, interpretations, representations (unless they are mind-independent), or agents. As it turns out, few accounts of computation satisfy this desideratum, but Copeland (1996) is a notable exception. The cost of the failure to satisfy such a desideratum is that paradigmatic computing devices computing in a world devoid of minds are impossible on such accounts. Put differently, failure to satisfy *Strong Objectivity* has ramifications regarding the extensional adequacy of an account.

Let us say that an account of computation satisfies *Weak Objectivity* if it it entails that whether a system is computational or not can be determined by a specific kind of intersubjective agreement. I have in mind the agreement generated by a critical social process along the lines of Longino (1990). Weak objectivity is not without teeth. An individual simply interpreting a physical system as being computational cannot make it so if the *Weak Objectivity* desideratum is respected.

4.1.2 Extensional Adequacy

An account of computation should certainly avoid pancomputation, but it should do better than that. An account of computation should classify paradigmatic examples of non-computational systems (e.g. rocks) as non-computational. Additionally, an account of computation should classify paradigmatic examples of computational systems as computational.[22]

4.1.3 Explanation

Again, in accordance with scientific practice, it is a matter of fact that we explain the behavior of certain systems in virtue of the computations that they perform. This is most obvious when we explain the behavior of a computational system in virtue of the program or computations that it is executing. An account of computation should provide us with resources to explain the computational capacities of a system in terms of computations.

Piccinini also draws our attention to the distinction between computational modeling and explanation. A computational model can be used to predict the behavior of its target system, but prediction is not explanation. Just because a system can be described or simulated by a computational model does not mean it is a computational system, the behavior of which is explained in terms of computations.

4.1.4 Miscomputation

Sometimes computation can go awry. They can go awry by delivering the incorrect input–output relations that at least partially characterize the computation. As Fresco (2013) points out, even when the correct input–output behavior is present, the computational process itself might go awry in other ways (e.g. if two bit flip errors canceled themselves out). An analysis of computation should

---

[22] For brevity, I have combined Piccinini's desiderata *Right Things Compute* and *Wrong Things Do Not Compute*.

be able to classify miscomputations of these sorts. There are a few different ways that one might characterize miscomputation.

Piccinini (2015, 14–15) characterizes miscomputation in the following way:

> As before, let M be a system computing function $f(i) = o_1$. Let P be the procedure M is supposed to follow in computing $f(i)$, with P consisting of computational steps $s_1, s_2, \ldots, s_n$. By definition, the outcome of s_n is o_1. Let s_i be the ith step in the sequence $s_1, s_2, \ldots, s_{n-1}$. M miscomputes $f(i)$ just in case, for any step s_i, after M takes step s_i, either M takes a computational step other than $s_i + 1$ or M fails to continue the computation.

Denote Piccinini's characterization of miscomputation as *Miscomputation$_P$*.

Note the phrase "is supposed to follow" in the definition of *Miscomputation$_P$*. This sets up some tension with *Strong Objectivity*. If an account satisfies *Strong Objectivity*, whether a system is a computing system cannot depend on minds. If "supposed to" derives from intentions of designers of artifacts, then there is obvious conflict. If "supposed to" follows from natural selection, then there is no conflict, but then *Miscomputation$_P$* could cover only natural computing systems and not artifacts, which would run afoul of *Extensional Adequacy*. *Miscomputation$_P$*, as stated, seems to leave room for accounts that satisfy only *Weak Objectivity*. It might be preferable to have a characterization of miscomputation to simultaneously satisfy *Strong Objectivity*, *Miscomputation*, and *Extensional Adequacy*.[23]

Here is an alternative characterization of miscomputation that avoids the problem:

> Miscomputation occurs when the probability that a system performs a computation is high, but the system fails to do so, where failure means incorrect output or incorrect intermediate steps.

Denote this characterization of computation as *Miscomputation$_D$*.

Importantly, this characterization seems to resolve the problem posed for Piccinini's characterization of miscomputation. There is no problem for attributing miscomputations in accounts of computation that satisfy *Strong Objectivity*.[24]

---

[23] Piccinini, in his own account, thinks that computational systems have a proper function associated with them, the function of computing in such and such ways, and this is how it is possible to satisfy *Miscomputation* and *Objectivity*. Whether this is successful depends on whether he provides an appropriately objective account of what a proper function is, which is something that will be discussed in Section 4.3.

[24] Samuel Fletcher has pointed out to me that if it requires a community to set a high value of probability, then it seems like Miscomputation$_D$ won't be compatible with *Strong Objectivity*.

This characterization of miscomputation can be read in two ways, depending on whether one thinks of probabilities objectively or subjectively. If one goes the objective route, then miscomputation will be as objective as the account of computation one uses to determine whether a system computes. If one interprets probability subjectively, then miscomputation can be more or less objective depending on the account of computation one accepts. There is a variety of different information that might inform one's subjective probabilities. Perhaps the system was designed to compute in certain ways. Perhaps it has been an agent's experience that it has computed in certain ways. Perhaps the agent knows that the system computes in certain ways under certain environmental circumstances, and the agent thinks those conditions are met or is less than certain that they are met. Whether a system is miscomputational or not depends on an agent's associated probabilities. Note: because this conception of miscomputation depends on an agent's probabilities, this means that miscomputation will be relative to agents. Let us stipulate that a system fails to compute. For an agent that attributes low probability to the system computing, the system doesn't miscompute; it just fails to compute. For an agent that attributes high probability to a system computing, it miscomputes. For agents that attribute neither high nor low probability to a system computing, then we might think that it is indeterminate whether there was miscomputation or failure to compute. So, this characterization of miscomputation makes it vague. This seems entirely reasonable. One might imagine, when engineering a new kind of computing system, that are cases where it is unclear whether a miscomputation occurs or not. Finally, systems that no agent has beliefs about cannot be categorized as miscomputing.

Both precisifications of *Miscomputation$_D$* seem reasonable candidates for a characterization of miscomputation that accords with our intuitions. Some might have stronger or weaker intuitions about whether miscomputation is a normative concept, and according to those intuitions they might prefer the objective or subjective formulations of *Miscomputation$_D$* accordingly.

4.1.5 Taxonomy

Different kinds of computers have very different capacities. An account of computation should allow for some kind of taxonomy to *explain* the different computational capacities of different kinds of computers. An account should help us distinguish between, for example, analog, digital, quantum, and hybrid

---

There are two ways to respond. First, is to characterize Miscomputation$_D$ as vague, but objective, like being bald. Second, is to characterize miscomputation generally as a fundamentally epistemic concept, as opposed to an ontological concept.

computers, among other categories. See Chapters 7, 11–13, and 16 in Piccinini (2015) for more on the differences between different kinds of computers.

4.1.6 Usability

If a physical process is a computation, it can be used by a finite observer, one that has a limited life span and limited cognitive powers, to obtain the desired values of a function. To head off a potential worry, it deserves to be noted that this does not conflict with *Strong Objectivity*. A physical process need not be *used* to be *usable*.

In order to be useable by a finite observer, Piccinini (2015, Ch. 15, section 2) requires the following conditions be met:

Executability A user must be able to prepare any input associated with a computation and be able to determine its outputs; the computational task must be characterizable independently of the putative computation; computations must be, at least in principle, repeatable; and the computing systems must be constructible in a broad sense.[25]

Automaticity Physical processes that institute computations do not require ingenuity, invention, or guesses.

Uniformity Any physical process that institutes a computation of a function need not be redesigned to accept different inputs.

Reliability A computing system must yield correct results at least some of the time.

The *Usability* desideratum is motivated by the concept of an effective procedure. The concept, as articulated in the last section, is essentially connected to what human beings can do *unaided* by anything but pencil and paper. The *Usability* desideratum forgoes that requirement. In fact, it is about what humans can accomplish when *aided* with physical systems that are *not* restricted to pencil and paper. That said, humans must have a certain kind of control over those systems in order for them to be useable to perform computations. Given that an account of computation is meant to take us beyond the concept of computation articulated by Turing, this seems like a very reasonable relaxation on restrictions.

There is a good reason for thinking that *Usability* is not an appropriate desideratum, at least as it is articulated above. When one does use it as a desideratum, a proper account of computation cannot deem any unusable system a

---

[25] I understand *Executability* to pertain to computation of functions or partial functions with finite domains.

computational system. This seems to be too strong. It would put us at odds with cognitive scientists who utilize computational descriptions to describe cognition broadly construed. For example, Marr (1982) provided a very influential computational description of the visual system, yet the visual system would seem to fail to meet the *Executability* subdesideratum of *Usability*. *Executability* requires one to be able to prepare all inputs to a system in order to consider it as computing a particular function. Of course, it seems absurd to suggest that one need to be able to prepare all possible inputs to the visual system in order to think about the visual system as performing computations. Marr's work seems to have established that it does regardless of whether it is executable in the sense under consideration. So, it is best to regard *Usability*, as currently worded, as sorting within the class of computational systems instead of as a desideratum.[26]

4.2 The Problem of Computational Underdetermination

Though not a desideratum identified by Piccinini, it is often considered important to solve the problem of computational underdetermination identified by Shagrir (2001). I will argue that requiring an account of computation to solve the problem of computational underdetermination is not an appropriate desideratum.

Piccinini (2008) provides a nice working example of the problem. Suppose that we consider a black box with two inputs and one output that can be represented by $f: \{0, .5, 1\} \times \{0, .5, 1\} \to \{0, .5, 1\}$, with the function defined as follows:

x	y	$f(x, y)$
0	0	0
0	.5	.5
.5	0	.5
0	1	.5
1	0	.5
.5	.5	.5
.5	1	.5
1	.5	.5
1	1	1

---

[26] Piccinini has suggested to me, in a private communication, that there is an extended sense of *Usability* that allows organisms to "use" processes performed by their brain. In this extended sense, there would be no conflict between Marr's theory of vision and *Usability*.

One can think of the computation, however it is effected, as a kind of averaging the inputs. Just because our system can be described by three input and three output states doesn't mean that it has to be described in this way. We might consider identifying the states currently labeled by "0" and ".5," and label both "0." Then the behavior of the device is described by the AND function.

x	y	$AND(x,y)$
0	0	0
0	1	0
1	0	0
1	1	1

Alternatively, we can identify the states currently labeled by ".5" and "1" and label both "1." Then the behavior of the device is described by the OR function:

x	y	$OR(x,y)$
0	0	0
0	1	1
1	0	1
1	1	1

Let us consider a slightly more complicated example with three of the above black boxes described by $f(x, y)$. The output of two of the boxes will serve as an input to another box. This setup seems perfectly computational, like a circuit. See Figure 3.

Of course, this very same physical system can be regarded as two black boxes described by $f(x, y)$ whose output is the input to box described by $AND(x, y)$. See Figure 4. An alternative description of the system would have all $AND(x, y)$ boxes or all $OR(x, y)$ boxes.

The problem of computational underdetermination is that physical systems are typically compatible with multiple computational descriptions (i.e. the inputs and outputs of a computer can be represented by a multiplicity of functions). Furthermore, the steps associated with a computation can be described in different ways as well. The problem of computational underdetermination is not nearly as bad, if it is bad at all, as the Putnam/Searle problem.

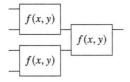

Figure 3 A computation where the outputs of two of the black boxes serve as inputs to another black box.

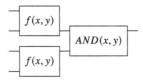

Figure 4 A black box computation where the outputs of two of the black boxes described by $f(x, y)$ are an input to a box described by $AND(x, y)$.

The Putnam/Searle problem is that every system computes everything and in any way. Computational underdetermination just indicates that for a particular system, there will generally be some different ways of characterizing it computationally, but these ways are significantly restricted.

It seems impossible to solve the problem of computational underdetermination while respecting the *Strong Objectivity* desideratum. For the black boxes above, we are free to describe the systems in any way that is useful to us. There is no sense in which any of the above descriptions is incorrect. Some descriptions used are coarse-grained, but using coarse-grained descriptions of systems is the stock and trade of science. Descriptions, in addition to being true or false, can be more or less useful to us depending on our aims. It seems reasonable to grant one the freedom to use any computational description of a system that suits one's purposes rather than insisting on one to the exclusion of others. In this case, when a system is computing, it performs all computations that true descriptions of the system would support, though we might typically be interested in one of those descriptions.

In the literature, it is generally understood that an account of computation that can solve the problem of computational underdetermination is desirable, but I fail to see what is at stake when it is unsolved. Furthermore, it is easy enough to explain why people have an *intuition* that the problem needs to be solved independently of any appeal to an account of computation. We live in a highly computationally connected society whose computational connections depend on shared conventions regarding computational descriptions. This widespread agreement is what suggests that there is a unique computational description of systems, even when there need not be. For these reasons, I do not think that having a solution to the problem of computational underdetermination should be a desideratum for accounts of computation.

4.3 The Mechanistic Account of Computation

Piccinini (2007) and (2015) have developed an account of computation that makes a significant break from other accounts of computation (see also Milkowski [2013]). In order to be a computing system, a system has to be a mechanism, in the sense of Machamer, Darden, and Craver (2000). Here is the mechanistic account (Piccinini, 2015, 10):

> A physical computing system is a mechanism whose teleological function is performing a physical computation. A physical computation is the manipulation (by a functional mechanism) of a medium-independent vehicle according to a rule. A medium-independent vehicle is a physical variable defined solely in terms of its degrees of freedom (e.g., whether its value is 1 or 0 during a given time interval), as opposed to its specific physical composition (e.g., whether it's a voltage and what voltage values correspond to 1 or 0 during a given time interval). A rule is a mapping from inputs and/or internal states to internal states and/or outputs.

There is a lot of terminology to unpack. A mechanism is a system consisting of a set of parts that have certain capacities. These parts of a mechanism are organized in a particular way, and this gives rise to the capacities of the entire mechanism. A functional mechanism is a mechanism that has teleological functions associated with it. "A teleological function [...] is a stable contribution to a goal (either objective or subjective) of organisms by either a trait or an artifact of the organisms" (Piccinini, 2015, 116).[27] Objective goals of organisms include survival and inclusive fitness. A computing mechanism is a functional mechanism that provides stable contributions to an organism's goal of performing computations. It should be noted that the components of a mechanism can have proper functions as well. A rule is just a mapping from inputs and possibly internal states to outputs. Input and outputs are realized by vehicles.

The concept of a vehicle deserves clarification, and one can do it by focusing on the fact that computing systems are mechanisms. Mechanisms are composed of a set of spatiotemporally located parts that have localized states associated with them, in addition to the global state of the entire mechanism. In this context, vehicles are states of some spatiotemporal parts of a mechanism that are processed when states of some spatiotemporal parts of a mechanism are

---

[27] Some might find an appeal to organisms surprising for an account of computation. Piccinini thinks that computers are particular kinds of functional mechanism, and in order to talk about functions, one has to implicate organisms.

changed. Some of the parts of a computing mechanism have the function of manipulating the states of parts of a mechanism in particular ways. Collectively, these parts ensure that the behavior of a mechanism can be described in terms of a rule.

A vehicle is *medium independent* when the rules for manipulating vehicles are functions of states associated with certain degrees of freedom and are insensitive to other degrees of freedom (122). Piccinini writes, "[A] given computation can be implemented in multiple physical media [...] provided that the media possess a sufficient number of dimensions of variation (or degrees of freedom) that can be appropriately accessed and manipulated, and that the components of the mechanism are functionally organized in an appropriate way" (122).

It is useful to consider a Turing machine in the context of the mechanistic account of computation. A Turing machine has a two-way infinite tape, a read/write tape head that can alter location, and a processor that updates states and controls the read/write tape head. The computational vehicles are the sequences of 0s and 1s on the tape. What is important is that these vehicles have two relevant degrees of freedom. First, there is the freedom to be 1 or 0. Second, there is their spatial distribution on a tape. These degrees of freedom can be instantiated in a multiplicity of different kinds of systems. The function of the read/write tape head is to read symbols and to properly update a state as well as to write and move in accordance to the processor. The arrangement and capacities of these individual systems allow the system to realize its function, computation.

Let us see how the mechanistic account of computation fares with respect to the desiderata considered in Section 4.1.

4.3.1 Objectivity

Part of Piccinini's account satisfies *Strong Objectivity*, but in total it does not. This is because of Piccinini's account of teleological functions. A system has a function when it makes a stable contribution to an objective or subjective goal of an organism or is the type of thing that does so. If Piccinini's account was restricted to only objective goals, it would satisfy *Strong Objectivity*, but otherwise it will not. Whether certain systems are computational depends on minds if it depends on subjective goals.

The account goes a long way toward satisfying *Weak Objectivity*. Whether a system admits a description as a computing mechanism is perfectly capable of being investigated in the right kinds of ways, at least to a significant extent. My hesitancy is with respect to determining whether a device has supported the subjective computational goals of an organism or not. While there are, no doubt, instances where there is evidence that a mechanism has supported the computational goals of organisms, there could certainly be cases where that evidence may be unavailable. We might imagine a group of computer scientists considering the mechanistic structure of a system and agreeing that it is a computer, but if it never has supported the goals of an organism, the mechanistic account cannot classify it as such. If a system or a member of its type never makes a stable contribution to the computational goals of an organism, it will not be computational.[28]

There is an easy fix for this problem. One might simply amend the mechanistic account so that it doesn't require that a system have a teleological function in the cases where the goals in question are subjective, but merely that the system or its type *could* provide a stable contribution to the goals of an organism.[29] In that case, Piccinini's account would certainly satisfy *Weak Objectivity* because whether or not a system *could* support the computational goals of an organism is certainly open to the kind of investigation associated with *Weak Objectivity*, thus resolving the issue.

This amendment comes with some consequences. If we assign functions to mechanisms based on the *capacity* to support computational goals of an organism, then, as described in Section 4.2, the very same system can support multiple computational goals associated with very different mechanistic descriptions of the system. It seems to me far better to satisfy *Objectivity* than to solve the problem of computational underdetermination for the reasons discussed in Section 4.2.

4.3.2 Extensional Adequacy

Subject to the modifications recommended in Section 4.3.1, it would appear that Piccinini does a fine job of isolating the right kinds of systems. His analysis seems to accommodate all paradigm examples of computers, even those that might be considered hostile to them, like measurement-based quantum computers (Duwell, 2017). Those kinds of computers are discussed in Section 5. Piccinini's proposal is less successful in avoiding classifying non-paradigmatic systems as non-computational systems.

---

[28] Piccinini has suggested to me that it is unlikely that judgments could be arrived at that a system could support the goals of an organism without actually attempting to perform a computation with the system. That may be the case, but the question is one of principle, as it always is when one provides a philosophical account.

[29] See Dewhurst (2018) for a fuller discussion of Piccinini's account of functions and possible friendly amendments.

Consider a meteoroid orbiting the sun. Here we have a two-body system that appears capable of being construed as a mechanism. To be a computing mechanism, it needs to process medium-independent vehicles. We can think of the computational vehicles being the position and velocity states of the meteoroid in question. Inputs to the system are the initial position and initial velocity of the meteoroid. Let us suppose that it is within our power to alter the position and initial velocity of the meteoroid so that we are able to satisfy *Usability*. The outputs are the later positions and velocities of the meteoroid. We know that there is a rule relating the inputs to outputs given by the laws of physics, and we also know that the rule is sensitive to variations only in a partial state of the system, not the total state. So, it looks like we have everything we need for a computing mechanism, except, possibly, the appropriate teleological function. If one had the subjective goal to compute the trajectory of this meteoroid, this system could certainly support that goal.

This example shows that the mechanistic account satisfies only extensional adequacy due to contingent circumstances. Systems like the meteoroid are taken as paradigmatically non-computational. It so happens that we don't use these kind of systems to complete computations. This contingent fact is the sole reason why, on the mechanistic account, these systems do not count as computers.[30] If someone were to use the system to compute, then the meteoroid would count as a computational system. The fact that it is unlikely that anyone will have such a goal seems beside the point. Someone could, and then that system would seem to meet all the criteria provided by the mechanistic account to be a computational system. If we accept the liberalization of the notion of function proposed above, then the above example would simply count as computational, and so would many systems that we simply don't think of as being computational. One might invoke *Usability* to help bring the mechanistic account more in line with *Extensional Adequacy*, but as I mentioned above, invoking *Usability* as a desideratum instead of a sorting mechanism runs into trouble with *Extensional Adequacy*.

There is a question about how serious this problem is for the mechanistic account. The Putnam/Searle problem got us worried about the extensional adequacy of an account of computation because if everything computes everything, then the concept of computation is trivial. It is important to emphasize that any worries about extensional adequacy generated by the above considerations are nothing like that. They don't come remotely close to trivializing the concept of computation associated with the mechanistic account.

---

[30] O. J. E. Maroney and Timpson (2018) argue that it is completely appropriate to have computational designations contingent on use.

In fact, the mechanistic account has some resources to make seeming violations of *Extensional Adequacy* less worrisome. The mechanistic account can characterize systems as being more or less computational within the class of computing systems it identifies. Systems like a meteoroid orbiting the sun can be considered to be *trivially* computational insofar as they have trivial computational explanations. On the other end of the spectrum, we have programmable computers such as universal Turing machines and the like that are anything but trivially computational insofar as they have very sophisticated computational explanations.

This suggests that perhaps the *Extensional Adequacy* desideratum ought to be augmented. It may be augmented so that an account of computation has to appropriately classify systems as either computational or non-computational, or appropriately classify systems as being more or less computational. Whether such an alteration is ultimately reasonable or not will not be pursued any further.

4.3.3 Explanation

The mechanistic account satisfies *Explanation*. By providing a mechanistic analysis for particular behaviors, one explains those behaviors, and in the case under consideration, those behaviors are explained in terms of computations. Every time a vehicle is manipulated in a computational mechanism, this counts as an individual computation. The totality of these computations explains the computational capacities of these systems. As mentioned above, when the number of primitive computations is very low, computational explanations are less interesting. When the number of computations is high, computational explanation can become very useful, precisely because of its medium independence. Medium-dependent explanations, while they may be highly valuable in certain cases, can be used on fewer types of systems generally.

Piccinini's account also has the resources to distinguish between computational modeling and computational explanation. Just because a system's behavior is described by a computational model, this is no guarantee that the system is a computing mechanism.

4.3.4 Miscomputation

One advantage that has been claimed for the mechanistic account is that it can provide an account of miscomputation, discussed in Section 4.1.4. Indeed, the mechanistic account satisfies *Miscomputation$_P$*. It can do so precisely because computing systems have teleological functions associated with them. Because they have these functions, one can say, without contradiction, that a computer is computing the value of a function at a certain point, despite the fact that that does not properly indicate the value of the function at that point, instead of saying that it cannot be computing that function at all.

The mechanistic account also satisfies *Miscomputation$_D$*. If a system supports a computational goal of an organism, it would seem that it would have to have high objective probability of performing the computation correctly. Furthermore, because it supports the computational goals of organisms, there would be reason for thinking that one would naturally attribute high subjective probability to successful computation. If a computation goes awry, these are the circumstances under which it would be natural to attribute a miscomputation to the system.

4.3.5 Taxonomy

Arguably, the greatest success of the mechanistic account is in terms of the resources it has to provide a taxonomy of computational resources. It offers a natural classification of different kinds of computers in terms of different types of computational vehicles. One of the most important computational vehicles is the digit. A digit is defined by finite set of states over a finite time interval. Digits can be transmitted from one spatial location to another and be concatenated either spatially or temporally. Digits of the same type are processed in the same ways by components of a computer. Other kinds of computers process different computational vehicles. For example, qudits are computational vehicles. These are d-dimensional quantum systems and are processed by quantum computers. Analog computers process analog vehicles that have a continuous degree of freedom that is manipulated in a computation. Neural computers manipulate neural vehicles, which are distinct from analog and digital vehicles (Piccinini & Bahar, 2013). A computer is hybrid if it uses different types of computational vehicle.

4.3.6 Usability

The mechanistic account is perfectly compatible with *Usability*. As mentioned in Section 4.3.2, the *Executability* subdesideratum of *Usability* would have the seemingly unfortunate effect of undermining the extensional adequacy of the account if one did add the requirement of *Usability* to the mechanistic account.

In Section 4.3 we have examined the mechanistic account of computation. The key insight is that computers have to be functional mechanisms of a certain sort. I think there is no question that this describes our computing artifacts (at least to date). It introduced the notion of computational vehicles and how they provide a useful way to classify different kinds of computational system. The view has some difficulties with *Objectivity*, but can be amended to deal with those issues quite straightforwardly. Systems that are otherwise considered non-computational could be computational on the mechanistic account. Even so, the mechanistic account has resources to classify certain systems as being more or less computational depending on the details of their mechanistic description. Finally, the account does well on issues related to explanation, as it can utilize the resources offered by the mechanistic account of explanations. It can also distinguish computational explanations from other kinds of explanations. Overall, the mechanistic account of computation is quite successful.

4.4 Abstraction/Representation Theory

Horsman, Stepney, Wagner, and Kendon (2014) introduced an account of computation, Abstraction/Representation (AR) theory, which has been subsequently developed (Fletcher, 2018, Horsman 2015, 2017, Horsman, Kendon, and Stepney, 2017, 2018, Horsman, Kendon, Stepney, and Young, 2017). The most important insight associated with AR theory is that our judgments about computation are mediated by the theories that describe the systems associated with computation.

Here is a simplified version of AR theory for performing a computation. A fundamental distinction for AR theory is between physical and abstract entities. Physical objects are associated with a set of physical "states" $\mathbf{P}$. The scare quotes are there because the term "states" typically refers to our abstract representation of systems or physical objects, not the objects themselves. Let us take similar liberties and denote the possible (physical) dynamics associated with physical systems by $\mathbf{F}$. A theory, $\mathcal{T}$, is associated with the physical computing system. It provides a set of states, $\mathbf{M}$ that represent $\mathbf{P}$ and dynamics that represents $\mathbf{F}$. The state that represents a particular physical system $\mathbf{p}$ is denoted by $\mathbf{m_p}$. AR theory requires that a theory associated with a computation has to be predictively accurate within a suitable tolerance for the computational task at hand, but that is the only requirement on that theory. It can be fine- or coarse-grained, so long as it is predictively accurate. So, $\mathcal{T}$ could be a paradigmatically computational description of a system or it could be a theory of physics. This allows for a multiplicity of descriptions with a particular system, and a multiplicity of computations that might be attributed to a system.

Horsman et al. (2018) introduce what they call a representation relation, $\mathcal{R_T}$, which they construe as a mapping from $\mathbf{P} \rightarrow \mathbf{M}$. They insist that physical systems represent abstract states. To be clear, this is *not* a mapping from our abstract representation of a physical system via a theory to other abstract states. "This inversion of the usual conception of representation is shown in the

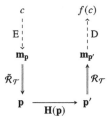

Figure 5 One encodes a point of a function, c, into a computing system by first relating it to states of a theory T that correspond to the computing system via E, and then initializing the system in that state. The computing system evolves. Then one measures a system appropriately to relate it to states in T, and uses D to relate the state to $f(c)$.

direction of its basic mapping; $\mathcal{R}_T : \mathbf{P} \rightarrow \mathbf{M}$, rather than an abstract object representing a physical one, $\mathbf{M} \rightarrow \mathbf{P}$" (31). Horsman et al. also consider a mapping $\tilde{\mathcal{R}}_T : \mathbf{M} \rightarrow \mathbf{P}$.

In order to evaluate a value of a function, f, one has to encode the point one wishes to evaluate the function at, c, into the computing system, and then suitably decode to recover $f(c)$. One does this via an encoding operation, E, which relates the domain of f and possibly f itself to abstract states of the theory we are using to describe the computing system. Encoding also involves checking that the computer is capable of representing the intended computation (137). Then, one uses $\tilde{\mathcal{R}}_T$ to set the initial states of the computing system in question. That system evolves in a certain way, denoted by $\mathbf{H} \in \mathbf{F}$, to the final (physical) state. $\mathcal{R}_T$ takes one from the computing system to its representation in T, and then one applies a decoding operation, D, to that state to recover $f(c)$. One can represent the process using the following equation: $D(\mathcal{R}_T(\mathbf{H}(\tilde{\mathcal{R}}_T(E(c)))))$ $= f(c)$. See Figure 5.

This characterization of computation has a fundamental problem in the way it characterizes representation relations involved in computation. Following van Fraassen (2006), it is a mistake to think that there can be a mapping from physical to the abstract. Mappings can only relate mathematical objects. As such, both $\mathcal{R}_T$ and $\tilde{\mathcal{R}}_T$ are ill-defined as mappings.

To correct for this problem, I propose a different way of characterizing $\mathcal{R}_T$ and $\tilde{\mathcal{R}}_T$. We can think about $\mathcal{R}_T$ and $\tilde{\mathcal{R}}_T$ as labeling representational relationships that obtain between physical systems and abstract entities (i.e. the states associated with a theory T instead of characterizing them as mappings). $\tilde{\mathcal{R}}_T$ can be thought of as the representational relationship between states of a theory and a physical system, where the states are the representational vehicles, and physical systems are the targets of those representations, which is perfectly straightforward. $\mathcal{R}_{\mathcal{T}}$ can be characterized as labeling a representational relationship between a physical system and states of a theory, where physical systems are the representational vehicles, and states of a theory are targets of the representation. This is a bit unusual, but it makes a good deal of sense in the context of computation. When we use a physical system to compute, the results of the computation are correlated with that physical system. We use the physical system to infer the result of that computation. How do we do so? With any predictively accurate theory of a system involved in a computation, there will be a procedure or set of procedures for associating states to a given physical system. In the context we are considering, measurement is one part of that procedure. Measurement represents the physical system of interest in particular ways that allow us to associate a particular state with it. We can then map from states to values of a function associated with the computation. That is the sense in which physical systems can represent abstract entities in the context of a computation.

Let us return to what the authors say about AR theory. Representation plays a crucial role in computation in AR theory. Some entity, **e**, must perform the encoding and decoding operations. Horsman et al. (2018, 19) write, "**e** [...] supports the representation relation $\mathcal{R}_{\mathcal{T}}$ it is using for **p**." It would be natural to think of **e** as using the representations associated with $\mathcal{T}$. The situation does not appear to be that straightforward.

In the case of a laptop computer, and presumably other similar devices, the user is considered to be the relevant computational entity (139). Consider the description of classical digital computers in (141):

Theory The theory of classical computing covers the hardware (including how the transistors implement Boolean logic, and how the architecture implements the von Neumann model) and the software (including programming language semantics, refinement, compilers, testing, and debugging).

Encode The problem is encoded as a computational problem by making design decisions and casting it in an appropriate formal representation.

Instantiate Instantiation covers the hardware (building the physical computer) and the software (downloading the program and instantiating it with input data).

Run The program executes on the physical hardware: The laws of physics describe how the transistors, exquisitely arranged as processing units and memory, and instantiated into a particular initial state, act to produce the system's final state when execution halts.

Represent The final state of the physical system is represented as the abstract result, for example, as the relevant numbers or characters.

Decode The represented computational result is decoded into the problem's answer.

Quite clearly, your typical computer user knows absolutely nothing of the theory associated with classical digital computing as described above in *Theory*. *Encode* claims that the encoding operation is associated with design of a computer, and certainly a typical computer user has nothing to do with such things. A typical user is involved in instantiation, which involves initial input data, or providing a command to execute a computation, but the user is not involved in building the computer or developing the software as in *Instantiation*. A user might launch a particular computation but is typically completely unaware of how their input affects the computing device in any significant way. With respect to *Represent*, the process is completely automated. Here the user plays no role whatsoever. Decoding does appear to be construed in line with earlier claims with a nontrivial role for a user. So, on AR theory, typical users of paradigm computers do extremely little of the work associated with *Instantiate* and *Represent*. The work done in determining how to coordinate states of a theory with physical systems clearly is representational work and requires a representational entity or entities, but those representational entities can quite clearly be separate from users of a computing system. Given the above considerations, it would seem that a typical user cannot fulfill the roles attributed to the representational entity associated with a computation, with *Encode* and *Instantiate* being clear barriers, though a typical user does perform some trivial encoding insofar as they select inputs and possibly a computation to perform. Furthermore, your typical user knows nothing of the theory T that AR theory deems essential to computation. So, it appears that in order for a system to be a computer, it needs not only a user, but other representational entities associated with it. With these clarifications, let us turn to the desiderata for computation.

4.4.1 Objectivity

In the absence of a naturalistic theory of representation, and the considerable difficulties associated with developing one (Frigg & Nguyen, 2020), one cannot claim with any seriousness that AR theory satisfies *Strong Objectivity*. It is possible for AR theory to satisfy *Weak Objectivity* insofar as there might be agreement that the requisite representational entities exist, agreement about a corresponding predictive theory, and agreement on how to associate theoretical states with the computing system. One issue is how one should make determinations regarding the encoding and decoding operations. Fletcher (2018) calls this the *objectivity problem for representational entities*.

Fletcher (2018) provides a critical analysis of AR theory and suggests that it is amended so that it has additional resources to meet *Weak Objectivity*. Fletcher calls this Agential AR (AAR) theory. AAR theory construes representational entities as agents. Fletcher takes agents to be entities with the following properties (459):

- Agents have access to or understanding of encodings, decodings, and representations.
- Agents are able to observe or measure the outcome of a physical evolution of a putative concrete computation to compare its result with that abstractly predicted.
- Agents have the ability (in principle) to gain evidence, hence confidence, about the validity of a theory concerning the objects involved in the putative concrete computation.

The reason why AAR theory cannot satisfy *Strong Objectivity* is that the above criteria for agents require them to have minds.

AAR theory does satisfy *Weak Objectivity*. Whether something has the above abilities is something that is open to scientific investigation, and there is a great deal of agreement to be had regarding which systems are agents in the intended sense. It is important to emphasize that, in AAR theory, to be an agent one does not have to have an understanding of encodings, decodings, and representations. The *existence* of such things in an agent's epistemic community and the in-principle accessibility of such things is what is required (Fletcher, 2018, 459–460). So, whether a system (including an agent) is computational or not does not supervene on that system alone, but on it and an appropriate epistemic community.

4.4.2 Extensional Adequacy

There is no question that AR/AAR theories will properly classify many paradigm instances of computation, but one wonders whether they misclassify others. Take an arbitrary paradigm computing device, like a laptop computer. If humans were extinguished by a terrible pandemic, as far-fetched as that seems, that device would no longer be considered a computer given that the requisite representational entities or agents are no longer present.[31] One way to address this issue would be to appeal to functions associated with computational physical systems, especially computing artifacts. An important question is whether an appeal to functions will make an appeal to representational entities superfluous, but I won't explore that possibility here. If one did add an account of functions AR or AAR theory, their extensions could be, at least in

---

[31] The mechanistic account doesn't face this problem because of Piccinini's account of functions. Once a system has a function, it is preserved whether the subjects whose goals it once supported are present or not.

principle, significantly different from the mechanistic account, which requires that computing systems be *mechanisms*.

One of the reasons that AR/AAR theories appeal to representational entities or agents is to address the Putnam/Searle problem. AR theory has significant difficulties with the Putnam/Searle problem. Given that AR theory requires representational entities in order for a system to compute, it is certainly not the case that every system computes. Furthermore, Horsman et al. (2014, 20) claim that encoding and decoding operations cannot be post hoc (i.e. occur after the putative computing system has already evolved). Yet, it appears that any representational entity could use the construction of Chalmers (1996) to interpret just about any system they want as computing just about anything nonetheless. Horsman et al. (2018) suggest that in cases like this the encoding and decoding operations are doing all of the work as opposed to the computer. That is certainly true, but it remains to be seen how one could systematically deal with the problem.

Fletcher intends AAR theory to fare better here. Regarding this, he writes (2018, 459):

> the only encodings, decodings, and representations that can be used in a legitimate concrete computation are those that are directly accessible, or comprehensible, to the agent. This rules out the many arbitrary encodings and decodings, as well as ones that, though not arbitrary, are too complicated to be immediately accessed, and similarly for representations.

So, on AAR theory, the inputs and outputs of a computational system need to be reasonably transparent to an agent in order for a computation to have taken place, as they are on the computers we use every day. This seems to be an effective means for addressing the Putnam/Searle problem. AAR theory seems to have a significant advantage over AR theory in this regard.

4.4.3 Explanation

AR and AAR, as currently developed, do not have much in the way of explanatory resources. Fletcher (2018, 454) has pointed out that AR and AAR theories draw our attention to the particular theories that provide the representational resources required for the representational entities so central to those theories. While it is certainly true that predictive theories of physical systems often afford explanations of the systems they apply to, that is true *generically*. Additionally, AR and AAR theory don't offer any insight into what makes an explanation of the capacities of a system *distinctively computational*. What AR and AAR theory can explain is why we can use certain systems to evaluate functions; but providing a computational explanation of those capacities entails providing an explanation in terms of computations.

The discussion of computer programs in Horsman et al. (2014) provides some suggestions as to how one could supplement the AR/AAR theories to solve the problem. If one thinks of a computer as solving a problem algorithmically, then it is associated with an effective procedure that draws on a set of primitive operations. Execution of a primitive operation is typically taken to be a computation. In the context of AR/AAR theories, algorithm execution doesn't have anything to do with a system being computational, so there needs to be some sort of legitimate way for associating steps of an algorithm to computations in AR/AAR theories. If a computational system has a set of subsystems associated with it, of which one could construct AR/AAR-type representations, like in Figure 5, for each of the components, and these components could individually be judged on AR/AAR theories as computing the corresponding primitive operations, then one could associate steps of an algorithm with the behavior of certain subsystems in a computer and thus explain the behavior of a composite computer in terms of computations executed by the component systems.

On the matter of distinguishing between computational modeling and computational explanation, AR and AAR theories have the resources to make the distinction. A computational model of a system would use a computer to represent that system. The system represented would not have to be a computer, and if it is not a computer, then presumably it wouldn't admit of a computational explanation.

4.4.4 Miscomputation

AR and AAR theory easily handle the *Miscomputation* desideratum. Recall that Miscomputation$_P$ occurs when a system is computing a function but fails to properly execute some step in the computation. There is an important sense in which the theories associated with a computational system have the resources to indicate miscomputation. Computation goes awry whenever the representational entities associated with it misrepresent the physical system meant to instantiate the computation. Misrepresentation might occur when the wrong representation is used for a physical system, or when the right one is used, but still fails to represent appropriately. It can occur at any stage in the representational process, preparation, evolution, or measurement.

AR and AAR theories fare well when we consider Miscomputation$_D$. According to Miscomputation$_D$, miscomputation occurs when there is a high probability of a system performing a computation, but the system fails to do so. Recall probabilities can be interpreted objectively or subjectively. It seems appropriate to examine Miscomputation$_D$ when probabilities are interpreted objectively in the context of AR/AAR theories. When we do so, we can see how a miscomputation can occur when the theory one used to represent the computational system in question has a limited domain of application, and the computational process takes place outside of such bounds. When we consider Miscomputation$_D$ from the point of view of subjective probabilities, AR/AAR theories again fare well. Here, an agent might assign high probability to successful computation because of their confidence in the theory that was used to represent the system.

4.4.5 Taxonomy

If one equips AR/AAR theories with an account of computational explanation based on algorithms, then they have no trouble satisfying the *Taxonomy* desideratum. One might show how a single system might support different computations in terms of which algorithms they are capable of executing. Furthermore, comparisons between systems can take place in terms of what algorithms they support. In comparing algorithms, one can compare different primitive operations different systems might be able to draw on. These primitive operations are a convenient way to sort between different classes of computers.

Analog computers satisfy algorithms whose primitive components manipulate continuous variables. Digital computers satisfy algorithms whose primitive components manipulate digital variables, those that can take on a discrete set of values. Quantum computers satisfy algorithms whose primitive components manipulate qubits, or qdits more generally. Hybrid computers would satisfy algorithms that manipulate more than one kind of variable.

Horsman (2015) claimed some success regarding the distinction between hybrid and heterotic computing systems. Hybrid computing systems are systems that utilize more than one kind of computational system. Heterotic computing systems are hybrid systems that have some computational advantage over individual components (Kendon, Sebald, & Stepney, 2015). Computational advantage is often understood in terms of temporal efficiency, but it need not be.

Horsman (2015, 13) offers the following characterization:

> If two physical systems **p** and **q** are elements of the representational triples
> $\langle \mathbf{p}, \mathcal{R}_{\mathcal{T}}, \mathbf{m_p} \rangle$ and $\langle \mathbf{q}, \mathcal{R}_{\mathcal{V}}, \mathbf{m_q} \rangle$, and individually satisfy all the requirements
> for being a computer, and if the joint physical system **p**∘**q** also participates in

the representational triple $\langle \mathbf{p} \circ \mathbf{q}, \mathcal{R}_\mu, \mathbf{m_p} \circ \mathbf{m_q} \rangle$ and satisfies the requirements for being a computer, if

$$\langle \mathbf{p} \circ \mathbf{q}, \mathcal{R}_\mu, \mathbf{m_p} \circ \mathbf{m_q} \rangle \neq \langle \mathbf{p}, \mathcal{R}_\mathcal{T}, \mathbf{m_p} \rangle \circ \langle \mathbf{q}, \mathcal{R}_\mathcal{V}, \mathbf{m_q} \rangle$$

then the computing system is heterotic. If the equality holds, then the computing system is hybrid.

Given the above characterization of AR theory, it is clear that the representational triples are meant to represent particular computational systems. For the hybrid and heterotic cases, we can assume that they have the same representational entities associated with them for convenience. There is a question regarding how to understand the inequality above. We know the inequality must somehow imply that the hybrid system has a computational advantage over its parts, in accordance with the fundamental difference between heterotic and merely hybrid computing that we started with. That said, Horsman does not provide us with any resources to help make that determination. Horsman does not indicate how the composition relation in the above inequality is to be understood. Remember, the representation relations associated with the symbol $\mathcal{R}$ are not actual mappings. So, the typical increase in conceptual clarity that is accompanied by deploying mathematical symbolism does not appear to be present in this case. Any claims of special success for AR theory in characterizing heterotic computing seem premature.

4.4.6 Usability

AR and AAR theories require that a computing system be used as a computer to be a computer. The encoding and decoding operations are essential to computational identity and require a representational entity to actually perform them in order for a computation to take place (Horsman et al., 2014, 15). One would think that this means that these theories would satisfy the *Usability* desideratum, but that is not the case. The *Executability* subdesideratum requires that in order to claim that one is computing a function, it must be possible for a user to prepare any input associated with that function. Neither AR nor AAR theories have such a requirement. Furthermore, the *Uniform* subdesideratum requires that any physical process that institutes a computation need not be redesigned to accept different inputs. Again, neither AR nor AAR theories have this requirement. These requirements would be trivial to add if one so desired.

4.5 Conclusions

This section began by considering the simple mapping account of computation, a perfectly reasonable first pass at an account of computation, but one that fails spectacularly nonetheless. Everything computes everything on that account. Any satisfactory account of computation must avoid this problem, but also do much more. Piccinini has provided an interesting set of desiderata for evaluating accounts of computation: *Objectivity, Extensional Adequacy, Explanation, Miscomputation, Taxonomy,* and *Usability.* I provided a critical discussion of those desiderata. I also rejected solving the problem of computational underdetermination as a reasonable desideratum for accounts of computation.

The first account of computation that was examined in detail was Piccinini's (2007; 2015) mechanistic account. That account makes functional mechanisms central to computation. This describes computing artifacts quite well. Piccinini's account has some difficulties with respect to *Objectivity* for putative computing systems that support subjective goals of organisms. These difficulties can be overcome by loosening up the account of functions associated with the mechanistic account, but this also raises some worries about *Extensional Adequacy.* The account certainly can provide a sense in which systems are more or less computational, which assuages worries about *Extensional Adequacy.* The mechanistic account does a fantastic job providing an account of computational explanation. Because computing mechanisms are functional mechanisms, the account has special resources for determining when miscomputation arises. The focus on properties of computational vehicles yielded a relatively transparent way to classify different kinds of computational systems. The mechanistic account does not satisfy *Usability,* but could easily be amended to do so.

The second cluster of accounts examined were AR and AAR theories. The most important insight of these theories is that our judgments of whether a system is computational or not crucially depend on a theory of the computational system. While this is surely a reasonably epistemological point to make, AR and AAR theories elevate this to a metaphysical requirement. Something isn't a computer unless we have a theory of the system and a system is used to compute. AR theory alone has few resources to satisfy *Objectivity.* AAR theory has significant advantage over AR theory in that regard. AAR theory clearly satisfies *Weak Objectivity.* AR and AAR theories have some challenges with *Extensional adequacy.* The requirement that computers need to be associated with representational entities raised serious questions about whether paradigm computational systems are recognized as such. AR does seem to be considerably worse off than AAR theory insofar as it had few resources to resolve the Putnam/Searle problem. Plenty of paradigmatic non-computational systems could be considered computational. Both AR and AAR theories can be equipped with resources to satisfy *Explanation.* AR and AAR theories handle

Miscomputation with ease. Given additional resources to develop an account of computational explanation, the theories could satisfy *Taxonomy*. Finally, the view can be made compatible with *Usability*.

This section was not meant to provide an exhaustive overview of accounts of computation.[32] My aim was to provide an overview that would give the reader a sense of the challenge, demonstrate how much has been accomplished, and indicate where there may be some work left to do. Most importantly, I hope that I've equipped the reader with conceptual resources for thinking about how computers might be implemented in physical systems. With that in place, we now have a look at the most exciting development in computing in the last thirty years, quantum computation.

5 Quantum Computers

In this section I will provide a brief overview of three prominent models of quantum computation: quantum circuit computers, measurement-based quantum computers, and adiabatic quantum computers.[33] These models indicate that quantum computation can be implemented in very different ways, serve as test cases to apply conceptual tools in the previous section and are crucial for considering why quantum computers are faster than classical computers, a topic that will be discussed in the next section. For a historical overview of the field of quantum computing and simple presentations of important quantum algorithms, see Hagar and Cuffaro (2019).

5.1 Quantum Circuit Computers

One of the most gentle introductions to quantum computation comes from comparing classical circuits to quantum circuits. The basic building blocks of classical circuit theory are classical bits, or *cbits*, and gates. Cbits are systems characterized by two *discrete* states, typically denoted by 0 and 1. They are to be contrasted with binary digits, which are numbers, not systems. Cbits are

---

[32] There are a host of other accounts of computation that haven't been discussed, which are worthy of attention, perhaps most importantly Copeland (1996). A non-exhaustive short list of more-recent contributions is Anderson (2019), Ladyman (2009), Rescorla (2014), and Schweizer (2019).

[33] Other models have been of considerable importance. Quantum Turing machines invented by Deutsch (1985) and developed in Bernstein and Vazirani (1997) were instrumental in providing a quantum complexity theoretic analysis of quantum computers, though not from the point of view of any practical realizations. Topological quantum computers are perhaps the most exotic quantum computers conceived, which utilize anyons for computation (Freedman, Kitaev, & Larson, 2003). They are of interest chiefly because of the possibility to minimize computational errors. The theoretical barriers to characterizing them are a bit too steep to consider here. See Lahtinen and Pachos (2017) for a reasonably gentle introduction to topological quantum computers.

systems that are typically used to represent the inputs and outputs of a circuit. Given the absolutely discrete nature of the possible states of cbits, the state space required to describe such cbits is easy to represent. The state of each cbit can be described by a binary number, and the state of all cbits can be represented by the Cartesian product of the individual states. So, an n-cbit system has 2^n possible states, each of which can be specified by n binary numbers. Measurement theory associated with systems of cbits is completely trivial. The state of an n-cbit system can always be determined with certainty. Finally, gates are systems that manipulate the state of cbits, either individually or jointly. Gates can either flip the state of a cbit or leave it alone, unconditionally, or conditional on the states of other cbits. This is exactly what we saw in Section 4 when we considered AND and OR gates.

Computations in the circuit model begin with some set of cbits in a fiducial state. They enter into the computer and get processed until some final set of cbits encodes the solution to the a computational problem. The fiducial state is utilized to keep track of the efficiency of a computation. Typically, cbits are taken to begin in the zero state. Manipulations required to prepare these cbits before they are processed by the computer may be factored into the computational cost associated with particular computational task.

Quantum circuits are analogous, but the situation is more complicated. The basic building blocks of quantum circuit theory are qubits and quantum gates. Qubits are individual two-dimensional quantum systems. The state of an individual qubit in a pure state can be written in the form $\alpha |0\rangle + \beta |1\rangle$, where $|0\rangle$ and $|1\rangle$ are computational basis states in the z-basis, and α and β are *continuous* complex parameters subject to the constraint that $|\alpha|^2 + |\beta|^2 = 1$. The mathematical framework used to represent individual qubits is a two-dimensional Hilbert space, a complex two-dimensional vector space equipped with the standard inner product and some other topological properties that are unimportant for this section. Pure states of individual qubits are represented by vectors of unit length centered on the origin.

One of the most interesting aspects of qubits is that the state of an n-qubit system cannot be represented by an n-fold Cartesian product of the individual qubit states. An n-qubit system is actually represented by an n-fold tensor product of two-dimensional Hilbert spaces. A state in that space in general requires 2^n *continuous parameters* to specify. The state of n cbits requires just n binary numbers to specify.

As is well known, measurement results for quantum systems are probabilistic. Some measurements are represented in quantum mechanics as a complete set of projections on Hilbert space.[34] The probability of getting a result corresponding to a particular projection is given by the complex conjugate of the inner product of the state vector of a system and the ray corresponding to the projection. To extract information from a quantum system, the output subsystem is measured in the computational basis. As long as the state of the output system is "close" to a computational basis state, such a measurement of the system will reveal that state with high probability. So, quantum computation tolerates some imprecision in the computational process.

The dynamics of a quantum system are represented by unitary operators on Hilbert space. Without going into detail, this entails that the dynamics is linear, reversible, and preserves inner products. The dynamics and tensor product structure of Hilbert space structure gives rise to the phenomenon of entanglement. A system is entangled if it cannot be written as a tensor product of pure states of individual qubits. A trivial example is the singlet state $(|0\rangle_A |1\rangle_B - |1\rangle_A |0\rangle_B)/\sqrt{2}$, of two qubit systems A and B, which cannot be written as a tensor product of pure states of the component systems $(\alpha |0\rangle_A + \beta |1\rangle_A) \otimes (\alpha' |0\rangle_B + \beta' |1\rangle_B)$.[35] The most natural reading of this fact is that the global properties of entangled systems are not reducible to the properties of the component systems. Entangled systems enjoy correlations unachievable with classical systems. Entanglement is a feature of quantum systems that makes them difficult to simulate classically (Josza and Linden, 2003).[36]

Dynamics in the quantum circuit model are instantiated by gates, similar to the classical circuit model. The action of the gates can be defined on basis states and extended by linearity for the rest of the state space. It has been crucial for efficient quantum algorithms that the gates that are utilized in the algorithms do not merely transform computational basis states into other computational basis states. A richer set of transformations is needed, but quantum computation does not simply help itself to all the dynamic transitions possible on quantum systems. Instead, it can be shown that there are certain sets of gates that are universal for quantum computation insofar as these gates in certain combinations

---

[34] This is far from being the whole story regarding measurement in quantum mechanics. For simplicity, the general theory of measurements is not discussed, but nothing is lost as it is not relevant for present purposes. See Neilsen and Chuang (2000), Chapter 2.2.3–2.2.6, for an introductory treatment of quantum measurements.

[35] A qubit state is mixed if it cannot be written in the form $\alpha |0\rangle + \beta |1\rangle$ where $|\alpha|^2 + |\beta|^2 = 1$. See Timpson and Brown (2005) for an illuminating discussion about pure and mixed states and how they relate to separable and inseparable states.

[36] Gross, Flammia, and Eisert (2009) have shown that too much entanglement makes quantum speedup impossible.

are sufficient to approximate any dynamic transformation possible to any nontrivial degree of accuracy (Neilsen & Chuang, 2000, Chapter 4.5).

Similar to classical circuit computers, quantum circuit computers begin a computation with some initial set of qubits in a fiducial state. Typically this state is taken to be the computational basis state $|0\rangle \ldots |0\rangle$. The gates composing the computer sequentially act on these qubits to produce a set of output qubits that encode the solution to the computational problem of interest.

It is useful to consider an example of a simple quantum computation that is a restriction of the Deutsch–Jozsa algorithm fully developed in Cleve, Ekert, Macchiavello, and Mosca (1998). The algorithm is used to check whether a function $f : \{0, 1\} \rightarrow \{0, 1\}$ is constant or balanced, where balanced functions are those that have the same number of 0s as 1s over their domain. Let the computation involve two qubits initially in the state $|0\rangle |0\rangle$ state. Flip one of those bits to get the state $|0\rangle |1\rangle$. Apply a Hadamard transformation to each bit to get the state

$$(|0\rangle + |1\rangle)(|0\rangle - |1\rangle)/2.$$

Notice, this takes the qubits out of their computational basis states to superposed states. At this stage of the computation, the qubits remain unentangled. Then suppose we have access to a unitary gate that instantiates a function f by acting on both qubits. The action of the gate is $|x\rangle |y\rangle \rightarrow |x\rangle |f(x) \oplus y\rangle$, where $\oplus$ denotes binary addition. If we apply it to the state of the system above, the system evolves to

$$(|0\rangle (|f(0) \oplus 0\rangle - |f(0) \oplus 1\rangle) + |1\rangle (|f(1) \oplus 0\rangle - |f(1) \oplus 1\rangle))/2.$$

The unitary interaction entangles the two qubits. If the function is constant, then $f(0) = f(1)$. The state of the system would be

$$(|0\rangle + |1\rangle)(|f(0) \oplus 0\rangle - |f(0) \oplus 1\rangle)/2.$$

If we apply a Hadamard transformation to the first qubit, the state becomes

$$|0\rangle (|f(0) \oplus 0\rangle - |f(0) \oplus 1\rangle)/\sqrt{2}.$$

Note the state of the first qubit. If instead the function is balanced, then $f(0) = f(1) \oplus 1$, and $f(1) = f(0) \oplus 1$. The state of the system would be

$$(|0\rangle - |1\rangle)(|f(0) \oplus 0\rangle - |f(0) \oplus 1\rangle)/2.$$

If we apply a Hadamard transformation to the first qubit, the state becomes

$$|1\rangle (|f(0) \oplus 0\rangle - |f(0) \oplus 1\rangle)/\sqrt{2}.$$

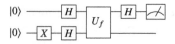

Figure 6 A circuit for determining whether a binary function is constant or balanced. The X gate is a bitflip gate. The H gate performs a Hadamard transformation. The U_f gate performs the transformation $|x\rangle\,|y\rangle \rightarrow |x\rangle\,|f(x) \oplus y\rangle$. Another Hadamard transformation is applied to the first qubit, thereby encoding the results of the computation, where the state will be $|0\rangle$ if the function is constant, and $|1\rangle$ if the function is balanced. Then the first qubit is measured to determine the results of the computation.

Note the state of the first qubit. So, if the function is constant, the first qubit will measure 0, and if it is balanced, it will measure 1. See Figure 6.

Notice that in this quantum computation, the gate that instantiates the unknown function, U_f, typically called an "oracle" gate, requires only one query. The computational cost of an oracle query is defined to be 1. In the classical case, in order to determine if a function is constant or balanced, one would have to use an oracle gate twice. It is understandable if the reader isn't shocked by the increase in efficiency associated with this restricted algorithm. The full Deutsch–Jozsa algorithm generalizes this result and demonstrates that whether any function $f\colon \{0, 1\}^n \rightarrow \{0, 1\}$ is constant or balanced can be determined with a single oracle query, while a classical deterministic algorithm, in the worst case, would require $2^{n-1} + 1$ queries (Cleve et al., 1998).

There are several points of comparison between classical circuits and quantum circuits to point out. First, quantum circuits can simulate classical circuits, simply by restricting the allowable dynamic transitions to those allowable in classical circuits. Second, though qubits are continuous systems, and bits are discrete, the power of the continuum is not exploited in quantum computation. If the states used in the computation were close (as measured by the inner product), the probabilities of success in an algorithm would alter slightly, but not enough to compromise the computation. That said, the above algorithm, and algorithms generally, make use of the possibility of quantum superposition and entanglement. Third, both classical and quantum circuits can be easily analyzed in terms of functional mechanism or in terms of the algorithms associated with each, but there are different models of quantum computation that don't dovetail so seamlessly with classical circuits. We now turn to a particularly interesting kind of quantum computer: the measurement-based quantum computer.

5.2 Measurement-Based Quantum Computers

Measurement-based quantum computers (MBQCs) are very interesting heterotic computing devices. They are composed of a two-dimensional array of entangled qubits, measurement devices, and a classical computer. Instead of using a series of gates to institute dynamical changes to qubits, MBQCs use measurement devices to institute those changes to qubits.

It is possible to efficiently simulate quantum circuits using MBQCs. As mentioned above, certain sets of gates are universal for quantum circuit computing. It turns out that the Clifford group gates, I, X, Y, Z, $\pi/2$-phase, Hadamard and CNOT, and any other single qubit rotation form a universal set of gates. Raussendorf and Briegel (2001) have shown how each of these gates can be simulated by coordinated measurements on an entangled set of qubits. It is useful to examine how an arbitrary single qubit rotation is enacted.

In order to enact a single qubit rotation, one requires a sequence of 5 qubits. The first qubit is considered the "input" qubit, and the fifth qubit is the "output" qubit. The scare quotes are in part because the qubits are static, but also for other reasons as will be described below. The qubits begin the computation with the input state being whatever it is, and the other qubits in a fiducial state. The qubits are then entangled with one another in a particular way. The qubits need to be measured in a particular sequence and in particular ways to get the desired effect. Let us suppose the input state is ψ. Let the rotation be characterized by Euler angles ξ, η, and ζ. Denote the desired output state by $U(\xi, \eta, \zeta) \, |\psi\rangle$, where $U(\xi, \eta, \zeta)$ is a unitary operator. Let s_i represent the outcome of measurement i, with $s_i \in \{0, 1\}$. A standard measurement is made on qubit 1. The outcome of this measurement and the rest of the measurements considered are random. A classical computer processes the results of this measurement and determines which measurement to use on qubit 2, which will be a function of ξ and s_1, and adjusts the measurement devices accordingly. Measurements on qubit 3 will be a function of η and s_2, and on qubit 4 a function of ζ and $s_1 + s_3$. After this process the final state will be $\sigma_x^{s_2+s_4} \sigma_z^{s_1+s_3} U(\xi, \eta, \zeta) \, |\psi\rangle$, where the σ_is are Pauli matrices. See Figure 7.

$\sigma_x^{s_2+s_4} \sigma_z^{s_1+s_3}$ is referred to as the "byproduct operator" associated with the computation. Note that σ_x is just a bit flip operation, and σ_z leaves $|0\rangle$ unchanged, but flips the phase of $|1\rangle$. This means that the final state is trivially related to the intended state. The classical computer that assists our quantum computer keeps track of these byproduct operators throughout the computation. Given that any σ_z^2 and $\sigma_x^2 = I$, the end result of accumulated byproduct operators will be to either flip the end results of the computation or to take it at face value. That is the sense in which the byproduct operators are computationally trivial.

As mentioned above, any circuit element can be simulated efficiently by a MBQC using a set of measurement patterns associated with the Clifford group gates and another single qubit rotation gate. We can conceive of a quantum circuit as a two-dimensional array of gates with a set of input qubits on the

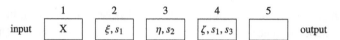

	1	2	3	4	5	
input	X	ξ, s_1	η, s_2	ζ, s_1, s_3		output

Figure 7 The measurement pattern for instituting an arbitrary qubit rotation characterized by the Euler angles ξ, η, ζ. The boxes and their arrangement represent a set of ordered qubits that are entangled. The measurements that are performed on the qubits are indicated inside the boxes. Measurements proceed sequentially from left to right, where the sign of the measurement angles depends on the results of earlier measurements. The boxed X is a measurement of the observable associated with σ_x. No measurements are made on qubit 5, which represents the output qubit.

left side that propagate through the gates until the computation is completed and we end up with a set of output qubits on the right side of the circuit, as in Figure 6. We can conceive of a MBQC as a two-dimensional array of qubits overlaying the circuit where measurement patterns are substituted for gates. So, the dynamic transformations associated with earlier gates are on the left, and dynamic transformations associated with later gates are on the right.

MBQCs have significant flexibility when simulating quantum circuits that is worth mentioning. Surprisingly, the temporal order of the gates one is simulating does not have to match the temporal order of the measurements on a measurement-based quantum computer. It turns out that all of the transformations associated with the Clifford group gates can be performed *simultaneously* and *initially*. This includes those qubits that correspond to input qubits as well as output qubits. Denote the set of qubits involved in the Clifford group gates as Q_1, the first set of simultaneously measurable qubits. Now, as we know from the example qubit rotation above, sometimes we need the results of certain measurements to know what the next set of measurements need to be to effect the desired dynamical changes in the system. Denote the set of qubits whose particular set of measurements depend on Q_1, as Q_2, and so on. So, the dynamical changes associated with a MBQC will be associated first with Q_1, then Q_2, and so on. See Figure 8. So, unlike the circuit model, nothing like the continual processing of input qubits occurs in an MBQC,

The mechanistic account provides some interesting insights into MBQCs (Duwell, 2017). Clearly an MBQC is composed of parts that have a particular spatial arrangement. It is composed of two interacting submechanisms, the classical computer, and the qubit array and corresponding measurement devices. Two different computational vehicles are used, classical digital vehicles as well as quantum vehicles. The classical vehicles set the initial measurement patterns and trigger the corresponding measurement interactions with quantum vehicles,

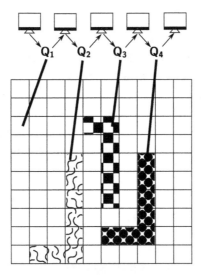

Figure 8 A MBQC. Each grid element represents a qubit. Differently shaded areas (including unshaded areas) represent sets of simultaneously measurable qubits. A classical computer sets the measurements for Q_1. These qubits are measured, and the computer keeps track of the appropriate byproduct operators and determines the next set of measurements for Q_2, and so on. A classical computer processes the final measurements and compensates for the byproduct operators to provide the result of the computation. Note, the depiction of the spatial distribution of simultaneously measurable qubits does not correspond to a real computation.

which alter not only the local state of the qubits measured, but also their global state. This alters the state of the measurement devices, generating a set of classical vehicles that are processed, and so on. So, the mechanistic account has no trouble with MBQCs. One might wonder whether it will handle the next model of computation so easily.

5.3 Adiabatic Quantum Computers

The basic idea behind adiabatic quantum computers (AQCs) is to make use of the quantum adiabatic theorem (Kato, 1950). The quantum adiabatic theorem states, very roughly, that if a system is initially in the ground state of a time-dependent Hamiltonian $H(t)$, then if $H(t)$ varies slowly enough, the system will remain in the ground state of $H(t)$. To exploit this feature of physical evolution for computational purposes, consider two Hamiltonians H_0 and H_1. Let the ground state of H_1 encode a solution to a computational problem. Let the time-varying Hamiltonian be $(1-s)H_0 + sH_1$, where $s \equiv t/t_f \in [0, 1]$, and where t_f is the time required to interpolate between H_0 and H_1 so that the system remains close to the ground state of H_1 at the end of the computation.

To get a sense of how the solution to a problem can be encoded into a Hamiltonian, it is useful to give a hint as to how Aharonov et al. (2007) proved that circuits can be simulated by AQCs. Suppose that the circuit we want to simulate is composed of n-qubits with L one- or two-qubit gates and that it begins a computation with all qubits in the $|0\rangle$ state. Let the state of the circuit after the l-th gate be $|\alpha(l)\rangle$. H_1 is chosen so that its ground state is a superposition of the entire history of the computation,

$$\frac{1}{\sqrt{L+1}} \sum_{l=0}^{L} |\alpha(l)\rangle \otimes |1^l 0^{L-l}\rangle .$$

$|1^l 0^{L-l}\rangle$ is a clock state composed of L qubits (Feynman, 1985). One can measure the clock state to check whether it is $|1\ldots 1\rangle$. If so, we can just measure the computational state and find $|\alpha(l)\rangle$. If we measure a different clock state, we simply repeat the computation and measurement process until we find the right clock state. This introduces a computational overhead, but one that is considered trivial.[37]

While the above method is general for simulating circuits, AQCs certainly need not proceed in this way. One might find different ways to encode the solution to a computational problem into the ground state of a final Hamiltonian, and choose initial Hamiltonians to minimize computation time.[38]

At first glance, one might think that a mechanistic description of AQCs is out of reach.[39] Their formal description gives one an impression of a group of qubits that simply evolve according to a Hamiltonian, which one might represent in their mind as being like a black box. In order to institute the kinds of Hamiltonians that one has in mind for AQCs, one needs a good deal of supporting computational architecture. For example, Harris et al. (2009) experimentally realized a limited AQC that utilized 8 compound Josephson-junction rf-superconducting quantum interference devices (CJJ rf-SQUID) to realize qubits and 16 rf-SQUID couplers to instantiate various Hamiltonians to alter those qubits. Certain components were the experimental realization of quantum computational vehicles, and other components had the function of driving

---

[37] See Cuffaro (2018) for a general understanding of what constitutes trivial computational overhead.

[38] See Albash and Lidar (2018, III. B.) to see a couple of different ways of implementing the Deutsch–Jozsa algorithm in adiabatic quantum computers.

[39] Sam Fletcher drew my attention to the fact that the mechanistic account of computation might have trouble with adiabatic quantum computers.

dynamic changes among them. So, it is pretty obvious that there are no barriers to considering mechanistic description of AQCs.

5.4 Conclusion

In this brief section we have examined three different models of quantum computation, all of which are computationally equivalent to one another. We have seen that while quantum computation can be made to look a lot like classical circuit computation, it certainly need not be. Now that we have a sense of what quantum computers are like, we can turn to the most important foundational issue in quantum computing.

6 Quantum Speedup

The reason why hundreds of millions of dollars have been spent on quantum computing is that quantum computers appear to be able to perform tasks significantly more efficiently than classical computers can.[40] Hints that quantum speedup was possible came initially from Feynman (1982). Later Deutsch (1985) showed that the best-case performance for some quantum algorithm was better than any classical algorithm. Deutsch and Jozsa (1992) provided a more sophisticated algorithm that could solve a problem in exponentially less time (as a function of input size of the problem in bits) than classical computers. It is safe to say that interest in quantum computing increased dramatically after Shor (1994) demonstrated that a quantum computer could factor large numbers exponentially faster than any known classical algorithm. Encryption systems typically depend on the *inability* of computing systems to factor large numbers efficiently. So, quantum computers, far from being of merely theoretical interest, became a pressing practical interest as well. As of the end of 2019, the Quantum Algorithm Zoo (https://quantumalgorithmzoo.org), which provides a catalog of quantum algorithms, indicates that there are 38 quantum algorithms that deliver exponential speedup over known algorithms, and 36 others with improvements over known classical algorithms.

The question that will be explored in this section is, what is the source of quantum speedup? While this is an interesting foundational question, it may also be interesting in practice. If one was able to explain speedup, then perhaps this explanation could serve as a guide to designing new, efficient algorithms that take us beyond what is achievable classically. Let us see what progress has been made.

---

[40] While this is certainly true in principle, it may not be true in practice. See Kalai (2020) for a pessimistic view of the possibility of building real quantum computers that exhibit speedup.

6.1 Computational Explanation

When we think about explaining quantum speedup, we want to pinpoint what makes a difference to the efficiency of a computation. How are we to find such a difference? Cuffaro (2013) and (2015) argue that we find such a difference by providing a certain kind of how-possibly explanation, one that appeals to the computational possibilities associated with quantum computers that are not associated with classical computers. Algorithms represent different computational possibilities insofar as they identify a set of possible computational paths depending on possible inputs or probabilistic transitions associated with those algorithms. In explaining quantum speedup, we are not interested in how-actually a particular instantiation of an algorithm is related to another particular instantiation of another algorithm.

As we have seen in the previous section, there are various models of quantum computation. This has some ramifications for explaining quantum speedup. Whether we are thinking algorithmically or mechanistically, the computational primitives associated with the circuit model of computation, MBQC model, and AQC model are very different. So, even when one is simulating a circuit that exhibits speedup on a MBQC, the particular computational explanation of the capacities of the circuit computer and MBQC will be different.[41] It would be conceptually convenient if it were possible to provide an explanation of quantum speedup that could be used for all models of quantum computation, but it is not clear that one exists.

What we are looking for is a trait shared by quantum algorithms that exhibit speedup. This shared trait, if it exists, will explain speedup only if it is not shared by quantum algorithms that do not exhibit speedup. In order to be practically useful, an explanation would provide some kind of heuristic that would facilitate the discovery of new, efficient quantum algorithms. The worry is that by trying to be as general as possible with an explanation of quantum speedup, we lose any heuristic value associated with the explanation. By sticking more closely with particular algorithms or models, then we might gain heuristic value, but lose generality. This is a fundamental trade-off that cannot be avoided.[42]

An example of the trade-off between generality and heuristic value can be illustrated by focusing in on a key process in some, but not all algorithms exhibiting quantum speedup. One such process is the quantum Fourier

---

[41] See Annovi (2015) for such a comparison.

[42] It deserves emphasis that scientific explanation is a deeply pragmatic activity. Certain explanations might serve certain purposes better than others. There is no reason to expect that a single explanation of quantum speedup can serve all purposes equally well.

transform. It plays a role in efficient quantum solutions to the factoring, discrete logarithm, and hidden subgroup problems, among others, but not in all algorithms exhibiting quantum speedup (Neilsen & Chuang, 2000, Ch. 5). That said, designers of quantum algorithms should keep the quantum Fourier transform in their minds as a tool that can be used if it is applicable to the problem they are trying to solve.[43] Explanations of speedup that exhibit this level of specificity can certainly be valuable, but let us see what can be done with more general explanations.

6.2 The Quantum Parallelism Thesis

The quantum parallelism thesis (QPT) is the thesis that quantum computers can compute multiple values of a function in a single step. Evidence for the thesis are processes like those in the full Deutsch–Jozsa algorithm. That algorithm takes a set of n qubits in the $|0\rangle$ state and submits each of them to a Hadamard transformation, putting all of them individually in the state $(|0\rangle + |1\rangle)/\sqrt{2}$. If we consider two qubits in this state, we see how they can represent several different numbers in superposition:

$$(|0\rangle + |1\rangle)/\sqrt{2} \otimes (|0\rangle + |1\rangle)/\sqrt{2} = (|00\rangle + |01\rangle + |10\rangle + |11\rangle)/2.$$

The right side of the equation above corresponds to a superposition of states corresponding to the numbers zero to three in binary. When we consider all of the qubits in this way, the state of the qubits is a superposition of all numbers from 0 to $2^n - 1$. The state is

$$\frac{1}{\sqrt{2^n}} \sum_{x=0}^{2^n-1} |x\rangle .$$

Note, n qubits were transformed using n Hadamard transformations into a state that represents numbers from 0 to $2^n - 1$. Refer to these n qubits as the input qubits. Also note that at this stage, the system is not entangled.

Now, adjoin an output qubit in the state $|0\rangle$ and submit the qubits to the following interaction:

$$|x\rangle |y\rangle \xrightarrow{U_f} |x\rangle |f(x) \oplus y\rangle \tag{6.1}$$

where $f: \{0, \ldots, 2^n - 1\} \to \{0, 1\}$ and $\oplus$ is addition mod 2. This interaction corresponds to an oracle gate, which computes the function of interest. Here is how the state transforms under U_f:

---

[43] Interestingly, Yoran and Short (2007) have shown that the quantum Fourier transform can be efficiently classically simulated. So, one cannot simply point to the quantum Fourier transform alone to explain speedup. There must be something about how the quantum Fourier transform integrates with the rest of the algorithm that is important for speedup.

$$\frac{1}{\sqrt{2^n}} \sum_{x=0}^{2^n-1} |x\rangle_i |0\rangle_o \xrightarrow{U_f} \sum_{x=0}^{2^n-1} |x\rangle_i |f(x)_o\rangle.$$

In a single computational step, it appears that all 2^n values of the function are computed. Because the qubits are entangled with one another, due to the action of the U_f gate, if we were to measure the system in the computational basis, it would reveal only one input-output valued pair $|x\rangle$ $|f(x)\rangle$ with probability $1/2^n$. So, the values of the function are largely inaccessible. If we wanted to make those values accessible, the results would have to be coded in accessible states, and the only way to do that would be to use an additional gate for every value of the function. This would require 2^n gates, as well as the additional qubits required to represent each value separately. If we don't take that trouble, can we claim that a process like this computes multiple values of a function in a single step?

Some have argued that there is a connection between the QPT and the many-worlds interpretation of quantum mechanics (MWI). Deutsch thinks that the only way to explain quantum speedup is by an appeal to computations happening in multiple worlds (Deutsch, 1985). Hewitt-Horsman (2009) has endorsed the QPT and claimed that the MWI has a special explanatory status with respect to it. Wallace (2012) agrees, though he doesn't make any claims that the QPT explains quantum speedup in all cases.

There is no reason to think that the only interpretation of quantum mechanics that can support the QPT is the MWI. Duwell (2007) argues that any interpretation that interprets pure quantum states ontologically will be able to endorse the thesis as much as any other.

Cuffaro (in press) maintains that explaining quantum speedup in terms of many-worlds is difficult for neo-Everettian formulations of the MWI that rely on decoherence to select a preferred basis to identify worlds, as in Wallace (2012). This is so because quantum computation depends on coherent super-positions. Because decoherence does not arise in the process described above, there is no way for a neo-Everettian to associate worlds with terms of the super-position involved in it. Cuffaro (2012) has identified an additional problem for MWI explanations of quantum computing. When one considers MBQCs, there certainly is branching due to measurement interactions, but those branches do not support claims about independent computational paths that correspond to individual values of a function being evaluated.

Some think that there are perfectly good reasons to think the QPT is false, and those reasons have nothing to do with any interpretation of quantum mechanics. Steane (2003) and Bub (2010) both maintain that computation of a value of a function requires that that value be accessible. Given that such values in processes like the one described above are inaccessible, the QPT is false.

Duwell (2018) has argued that much of the disagreement regarding the QPT is largely about vocabulary regarding what constitutes a computation, and that a more neutral formulation of the thesis is helpful. Consider the following formulation:

QPT′ A quantum computer can generate a system in a state correlated to multiple values of a function in a single computational step.

The QPT′ seems uncontroversial and has the explanatory power that advocates of the QPT are looking for. Having such a state enables one to extract some global information about a function that would seem otherwise difficult to extract efficiently.

One might reasonably worry whether the QPT′ can apply to MBQCs. There are subtleties associated with thinking about oracles with respect to MBQCs. When an MBQC is simulating a quantum circuit that has an oracle, there is nothing really like a single step through which it does so. All of the general temporal flexibility a MBQC has in simulating a regular gate applies to oracles too. Duwell has argued that once such subtleties are taken into account, we can use the QPT′ to explain MBQCs as well. According to him, the appropriate analog to the QPT′ in this case is an oracle free (OF) version of QPT′ :

OF-QPT′ A quantum computer can generate a system in a state correlated to multiple values of a function in exponentially fewer steps than a classical computer can.

One might object that this is a restatement of quantum speedup, not an explanation of it. It isn't a restatement of quantum speedup because OF-QPT′ does not solely claim that a quantum computer solves a problem in exponentially fewer steps than a classical computer. Instead, it focuses on the efficient generation of a particular kind of correlation, a correlation between a state of a computer and all values of a function. Note, classical algorithms for determining whether a function is constant or balanced do not reach such a state. At most, classical algorithms require $2^{n-1} + 1$ oracle queries, so their state is never correlated to all values of the function one seeks information about. The ability for quantum computers to reach states correlated to all values of a function efficiently seems crucial to explain speedup.

One might also reasonably worry whether the QPT′ can apply to AQCs. If one follows the general scheme for simulating circuit computers mentioned in the previous section, then one slowly, but not too slowly, turns on a Hamiltonian with a ground state of the form

$$\frac{1}{\sqrt{L+1}} \sum_{l=0}^{L} |\alpha(l)\rangle \otimes |1^l 0^{L-l}\rangle \, .$$

Recall that $|\alpha(l)\rangle$ is the state of the circuit computer at the l-th stage of the computation. So, the ground state of that Hamiltonian is correlated with the state of a circuit after the evaluation of an oracle gate. Yet, recall that one takes an adiabatic and continuous path to that ground state from the initial state. That makes it seemingly impossible to describe the computation in terms of computational steps, a clear obstacle to the application of the QPT in any of its versions above.

One might try to substitute "time" for "steps" in the OF-QPT′, coming up with an "adiabatic" QPT′:

A-QPT′ A quantum computer can generate a system in a state correlated to multiple values of a function in exponentially less time than a classical computer can.

Another problem arises. Granted, the A-QPT′ applies in some adiabatic algorithms, when the explicit simultation procedure above is used. That said, there exist some algorithms whose implementation is more direct, but they don't feature a state correlated to all values of a function. The adiabatic algorithm for Grover's algorithm comes to mind. The problem can be stated quite clearly without going into the details of the algorithm. Grover's algorithm is a search algorithm. It finds a particular entry in an unstructured list. We can think about a search in a list for an entry, m, by representing it as a function f, where $f(m) = 1$ and for $x \neq m, f(x) = 0$. Grover's algorithm on a circuit computer ends up evaluating this function for all x. Following Roland and Cerf (2002), it is convenient to choose a final Hamiltonian for our AQC to be $I - |m\rangle \langle m|$. So, nowhere does there appear anything like f-dependence on the state of the computer. There is only dependence of the state on the final value of the function. Yet, even in this instance it is difficult to thwart the A-QPT′. There is a hidden f-dependence in the Hamiltonian that one interpolates to in Grover's algorithm. One might write the Hamiltonian in a different form, as $I - \sum_x f(x) |x\rangle \langle x|$. This will be equal to $I - |m\rangle \langle m|$ because only $f(m)$ is nonzero. So, again, the requisite f-dependence for an application of the A-QPT′ is possible.

A final objection is worth considering. The Hamiltonian one is interpolating to in adiabatic algorithms will have f-dependence, and such f-dependence on the state of the computer will appear as soon as the algorithm begins, but one cannot extract any useful information with that kind of state early in the computational process. So, the A-QPT′ isn't explanatory. I don't think that this means that the A-QPT′ isn't explanatory. Instead, I think it simply indicates that it alone, along with other versions of the QPT′, cannot effect a *complete* explanation of speedup.

Bub (2010) has seen this quite clearly. Though he doesn't put it in these words, the truth of some version of a QPT′ won't get the job done. One has to show how one can extract useful information from such states efficiently when one doesn't have access to the values of the function.

6.3 Bub's Quantum-Logical Approach

Bub (2010) examines the restricted Deutsch–Jozsa algorithm considered above, Simon's algorithm, and Shor's algorithm, finding ways in which information can be extracted depending on the computational task at hand. Let's consider the restricted Deutsch–Jozsa algorithm from Bub's point of view.

There are four possible functions $f : \{0, 1\} \rightarrow \{0, 1\}$: $f(x) = 0, f(x) = 1$, $f(x) = x, f(x) = x \oplus 1$. Balanced functions correspond to a disjunction of $f(x) = x$ and $f(x) = x \oplus 1$, and constant functions correspond to a disjunction of $f(x) = 0$ and $f(x) = 1$. In classical logic, in order to make a disjunction true, one would have to have at least one of the disjuncts be true. If we think about classical circuits performing such a computation, then a disjunct would be true by evaluating *both* values of the function. Any *single* evaluation of the function is compatible with either disjunction being true (e.g. $f(0) = 0$ is compatible with $f(x) = 0$ or $f(x) = x$, one a constant function, the other balanced). In quantum logic, disjunctions are represented by subspaces. As we have seen in Section 5.1, one can choose an intelligent encoding of the problem so that the final state of the quantum computer ends up in one of two orthogonal subspaces, depending on whether the function of interest is constant or balanced. We decide which disjunction of functions is true by making a measurement that distinguishes those subspaces. Interestingly, the state can be in one of those two subspaces without needing to be such that all the values of a function can be extracted.[44] If one wanted to extract that information from quantum computers, they would require the same number of evaluations of the function as in the classical case. Bub makes similar points about Simon's algorithm and Shor's algorithm.

Simon's algorithm and Shor's algorithm both involve the evaluation of periods. Bub writes (237):

---

[44] One might characterize this situation by claiming that in quantum mechanics a disjunction may be true without any of the disjuncts being true.

Since f is periodic, the possible outputs of f – the values of f for the different inputs – partition the set of input values into mutually exclusive and collectively exhaustive subsets, and these subsets depend on the period. So, determining the period of f amounts to distinguishing the partition corresponding to the period from alternative partitions corresponding to alternative possible periods.

Simon's algorithm and Shor's algorithm are efficient because they encode these partitions into subspaces with minimal overlap. Again, the state of a quantum computer can be in one of the subspaces without needing to be such that all the values of a function within each period can be extracted.

Bub explains speedup in the Deutsch–Jozsa algorithm, Simon's algorithm, and Shor's algorithm by the fact that one can represent different propositions regarding the global properties of a function using largely nonoverlapping subspaces, but one cannot do anything like that classically. Representing such propositions classically involves generating accessible values of the function, which is more resource intensive.

Bub's explanation of quantum speedup is illuminating because it points to ways that one can encode information in quantum systems differently than one can in the classical case. This encoding allows access to global information of a function without access to the individual values of a function. I view Bub's explanation as a useful addition to the explanatory power of versions of the QPT′. There are other aspects of quantum speedup that are useful to draw attention to as well.

6.4 Speedup-able problems

Aaronson and Ambainis (2014, 134) write that the central lesson of quantum algorithm research is, "Quantum computers can offer superpolynomial speedups over classical computers, but only for certain 'structured' problems." As was evident from our discussion of quantum parallelism, one cannot simply extract all the information from a function efficiently, even if one generates a state correlated to all values of a function efficiently. One can instead extract some kind of global information from the function if one has some kind of knowledge about the function (e.g. whether it is constant or balanced). Not all problems are structured, like the search problem that Grover's algorithm deals with, and in such cases superpolynomial speedups are not possible (Beals, Buhrman, Cleve, Mosca, & de Wolf, 2001; Bennett, Bernstein, Brassard, & Vazirani, 1997). Let us examine an interesting result.

STRUCTURE AND SPEEDUP

Suppose that $f, g : \mathbb{N} \rightarrow \mathbb{N}$. $f \in O(g)$ if there are numbers $c, d \in \mathbb{N}$ such that $f(n) \leq c \cdot g(n)$ for all $n \geq d$ (Vollmer 1999, 234).

In what follows I utilize the notation used in Aaronson and Ambainis (2014). Let $f : [M]^N \rightarrow \{0, 1, *\}$, where $*$ indicates the input is outside of the "domain" of f, which we label by S, where $S \subset [M]^N$. Note, for binary functions $M = 2$, and so on. Let $R(f)$ be the expected number of queries made by an optimal randomized algorithm that, for every $X \in S$, computes $f(X)$ with probability at least 2/3. $Q(f)$ is defined similarly, but for quantum algorithms. Aaronson and Ambainis (2014) define *permutation invariance* in the following way:

A partial function $f : [M]^N \rightarrow \{0, 1, *\}$ is *permutation-invariant* if $f(x_1, \ldots, x_N) = f(\tau(x_{\sigma(1)}), \ldots \tau(x_{\sigma(N)}))$ for all inputs $X \in [M]^N$ and all permutations $\sigma \in S_N$ and $\tau \in S_M$.

Finally, Aaronson and Ambainis (2014) prove the following regarding permutation invariance:

$R(f) = O(Q(f)^7 \text{polylog} Q(f))$ for every partial function $f : [M]^N \rightarrow \{0, 1, *\}$ that is permutation-invariant.

So, given a certain structure, permutation invariance, one can prove that certain relations exist between quantum and classical models.

It is beyond the scope of this Element to provide a comprehensive assessment of the status of such investigations. See Ambainis (2019) for an overview. What can be said is that a general study of the structure of problems that are speedup-able could provide a useful tool for theoreticians aiming to discover new algorithms. Furthermore, an appeal to the structure of problems is generally explanatory. It makes a difference to whether speedup is possible or not. The techniques for extracting the desired information from structured problems will be varied but will probably involve interference.

6.5 Interference

Many have suggested that interference is crucial for extracting information from algorithms (e.g. Cleve et al. [1998] and Bennett and DiVincenzo [2000]). Fortnow (2003) makes an interesting case for thinking that interference effects separate quantum and classical computers generally. He finds an interesting matrix representation of both classical and quantum computers and then simply points to the difference between those representations.

Fortnow focuses on probabilistic Turing machines as a representation of classical computers, and quantum Turing machines as a representation of quantum computers. Recall that the action of a conventional Turing machine is determined by its machine table, which has entries of the form $\langle q_i, s_i, q_j, s_j, d\rangle$, which indicates how to change from configuration i to configuration j. Probabilistic Turing machine tables specify transition probabilities for such changes. Fortnow represents probabilistic Turing machines by a matrix whose rows and columns correspond to different possible machine configurations. The matrix entry, $T(c_i, c_j)$, is defined as the probability that the computer goes from c_i to c_j in a single step. The probability that the computer will go from c_i to c_j in t steps is $T^t(c_i, c_j)$. There are some interesting results that can be had with these matrices.

Let c_0 be the initial configuration of a probabilistic Turing machine, c_f a final configuration, and t be polynomially related to the input size. We have the following results. Fortnow claims that if L is in complexity class **BPP**, then there exists a matrix T as described above and a polynomial t such that if $x \in L$, then $T^t(c_0, c_f) \geq 2/3$, and if $x \notin L$, then $T^t(c_0, c_f) \leq 1/3$. **BPP** represents that class of languages for which there exists a polynomial time probabilistic Turing machine that will indicate whether an element x is in a language (accept) with probability greater than 2/3 or indicate that it is not in a language (reject) with probability greater than 2/3.[45] One might wonder how deciding whether a string is in a language is related to any problem we might want to solve. Cuffaro (2013) offers the useful example of checking whether a number is prime, where we have some string x, and we check whether it is L, which consists of the set of prime numbers.[46]

Fortnow represents quantum Turing machines in a similar way, but makes three significant changes. He allows matrix entries to be negative, requires that the matrices be unitary, and $T^t(c_i, c_j)^2$ is the probability to get from c_i to c_j in t steps. Fornow claims that if L is in **BQP**, then there exists a T as described above and a polynomial t such that if $x \in L$, then $T^t(c_i, c_j)^2 \geq 2/3$, and if $x \notin L$,

---

[45] I've used 2/3 in the definition of **BPP**, but probability greater than $1/2 + n^k$, with k a constant, will do (Cuffaro, 2018).

[46] Cuffaro (2018) is an excellent source of insight into complexity theory generally. See Aaronson (2011) for some thoughts about relations between complexity classes and the problems that define them. Finally, Dean (2016) provides a compact overview of complexity theory and contains definitions of many important complexity classes.

then $T'(c_0, c_f)^2 \leq 1/3$. **BQP** is the set of languages for which there exists a polynomially bounded quantum Turing machine that indicates if a string is in a language (accept) with probability greater than 2/3 or indicates that it is not in a language (reject) with probability greater than 2/3.

Fortnow takes the crucial difference between classical and quantum computers to be that quantum computers allow for interference effects. Certain computational paths can be associated with negative numbers and hence cancel other computational paths, but that's not true in the classical case.

In a further development, physicists have begun quantifying interference. Braun and Georgeot (2006) develop a measure that satisfies a number of intuitive properties and have shown that Grover's algorithm and Shor's algorithm use interference to different degrees. Interestingly, Grover's algorithm uses a low amount of interference and achieves only a quadratic speedup over a corresponding classical algorithm, and Shor's algorithm uses an exponential amount of interference and achieves an exponential speedup. Braun and Georgeot (2008) show that if one destroys interference via the introduction of errors in the computational process, the probability of success in Grover's and Shor's algorithms decreases. It would be quite fascinating to see how these apply to quantum algorithms generally, to see if amount of interference correlates to amount of speedup.

There is disagreement in the literature over what the proper measure of interference might be. Stahlke (2014) has developed a different measure of interference and has shown that algorithms with a low degree of interference can be classically simulated. Right now, quantification of interference is in its infancy. It will be interesting to see how measures of interference might develop, and to see what results might come from it.

6.6 Entanglement

There are significant reasons for thinking that quantum entanglement is partially explanatory of quantum speedup. It is obviously a feature that separates quantum from classical systems, and it is also a feature that arises in almost all quantum algorithms that have exhibited speedup. Furthermore, it is because of entanglement that an n-qubit system has exponentially many degrees of freedom associated with it, and an n-cbit system does not. Those "extra" degrees of freedom are associated with entangled states. So, one gets exponentially more degrees of freedom using the same number of resources. Furthermore, the energy resources associated with accessing those degrees of freedom is linear in n. Ekert and Jozsa (1998) have pointed out that one might attempt to compute with a single system with 2^n degrees of freedom, but then the energy required

The Philosophy of Physics

to access those states scales exponentially. So, there is something very special about entanglement with respect to the degrees of freedom it affords, and the spatial and energetic resources required to access those degrees of freedom.[47] Ekert and Jozsa (1998) argued that access to entanglement is what drives the efficiency of the quantum Fourier transform, which, as mentioned above, plays a crucial role in many quantum algorithms that exhibit speedup. Furthermore, entanglement is often required to generate a state correlated to all values of a function that one seeks to extract some global information from. Additionally, Josza and Linden (2003) demonstrated that entanglement is necessary for quantum speedup utilizing pure states. So, why not think that entanglement is always *explanatory* of quantum speedup, at least in the case of pure states?

Josza and Linden (2003) proved that if one has a polynomial time quantum circuit that utilizes two-qubit gates on pure states, and if at each step of the computation groups of no more than p qubits are entangled, for p an integer, then the circuit can be efficiently simulated classically by tracking the coefficients associated with the states in the quantum computation.[48] This shows that unbounded multipartite entanglement is necessary for exponential pure state quantum speedup. If there is an exponential quantum speedup, then it must be the case that there is no efficient simulation of the usual states of the corresponding quantum algorithm by tracking the coefficients at each stage of the algorithm. By the contrapositive of Jozsa and Linden's result, the quantum algorithm utilizes unbounded multipartite entanglement.

Jozsa and Linden are careful to point out that this doesn't mean that unbounded multipartite entangled states cannot be efficiently simulated. If one is going to simulate them efficiently, one has to do it in a different way than keeping track of the coefficients of the usual states. The Gottesman–Knill theorem demonstrates that there is a class of quantum gates whose action on quantum states can be efficiently classically simulated, but it is not simulated by keeping track of the coefficients associated with the usual states. Instead, a different formalism is used, the so-called stabilizer formalism, to do so. It turns out that the gates associated with the Gottesman–Knill theorem can generate unbounded multipartite entanglement. So, just because an algorithm cannot be simulated classically by tracking the coefficients associated with the usual state

---

[47] See Lloyd (1999) for interesting ways to compute searches that exceed standard classical computational efficiencies without entanglement, but by incurring an additional resources cost over quantum computers.

[48] To clarify, if a computation takes place on n qubits, Jozsa and Linden require that these qubits can be partitioned into subsets of at most size p after every computational step, and any multipartite entanglement is confined within these partitions.

at every stage, it does not mean that there exists no efficient way to simulate a quantum computer that does utilize unbounded multiparticle entanglement.

Some have suggested that the significance of the Gottesman–Knill theorem is that entanglement, even unbounded multipartite entanglement, is not sufficient for quantum speedup (Datta, Flammia, & Caves, 2005; Neilsen & Chuang, 2000). While this is true, it deserves to be qualified. Cuffaro (2013) and (2017) have argued that entanglement is sufficient to *enable* quantum speedup. Cuffaro points out that Gottesman–Knill operations generate states that admit of a locally causal description, hence a classical description. It is unsurprising that they can be efficiently simulated classically. So in order for multipartite entanglement to be sufficient to enable superpolynomial quantum speedup, and also explain that speedup, it will have to involve entangled states that do not admit of a locally causal description.

Even if the Gottesman–Knill theorem is no challenge to an appeal to entanglement to explain quantum speedup, there are other challenges. Meyer (2000) has shown that the Bernstein–Vazirani algorithm utilizes no entanglement. This result doesn't run afoul of Jozsa and Linden's results because the algorithm appears to offer only a linear speedup instead of an exponential one, which would necessarily involve unbounded multipartite entanglement. So, if the Bernstein–Vazirani algorithm is an instance of quantum speedup, and it appears to be, then even if entanglement is explanatory in some cases of quantum speedup, it isn't explanatory of them all. There are other challenges.

It is useful to consider some new results established in Johansson and Larsson (2017) and (2019). Johansson and Larsson's work draws on Spekkens' toy theory (Spekkens, 2007). Spekkens' toy theory shows that one can qualitatively reproduce a rather stunning array of seemingly quantum phenomena by a theory that has completely ontic states, but is restricted in terms of the knowledge one can have of those states. Johansson and Larsson extend Spekkens' work to develop what they call Quantum Simulation Logic (QSL). QLS represents qubits using two bits instead of one, thus corresponding to computational degrees of freedom ($|0\rangle$ or $|1\rangle$), but also phase freedom $((|0\rangle + |1\rangle)/\sqrt{2}$ or $(|0\rangle - |1\rangle))/\sqrt{2}$. It turns out that equipping systems with this additional degree of freedom has some fascinating features. Johansson and Larsson show that QLS can match the oracle efficiency associated with the Bernstein–Vazirani algorithm, the Deutsch–Jozsa algorithm, and Simon's algorithm, all three of which have been associated with quantum speedup. Josza and Linden (2003) have argued that Simon's algorithm utilzies unbounded multipartite entanglement. It should be emphasized that the oracle that QLS use for their results is not an oracle that would be associated with a classical computer. For that reason, Johansson and Larsson's claims that efficient QLS algorithms show that there is an efficient classical simulation of the algorithms mentioned above are simply false. Ironically, if they were correct about their claims that QSL algorithms have efficient classical simulations, which they are not, then they would have demonstrated that neither the Bernstein–Vazirani, Deutsch–Jozsa, nor Simon's algorithms demonstrate quantum speedup. So, their results would tell us absolutely nothing about what explains quantum speedup.

That aside, the fact that there are QSL algorithms that can reproduce the efficiency of a quantum algorithms is interesting. Johansson and Larsson write (2019, 69):

> In conclusion, the enabling root cause (resource) for the quantum speed-up in the mentioned examples [Bernstein-Vazirani, Deutsch-Jozsa, and Simon's algorithms] is not superposition, interference, entanglement, contextuality, the continuity of quantum state space, or quantum coherence. It is the ability to store, process, and retrieve information in an additional information-carrying degree of freedom in the physical system being used as information carrier.

This conclusion seems hasty for several reasons. First, we need to steer clear of the simulation fallacy. The simulation fallacy is to improperly read off features of the simulation as properties of the thing simulated (Timpson, 2013). So, if a QSL algorithm simulates a quantum algorithm, and the QSL algorithm achieves its efficiency one way, it does not entail that the quantum algorithm achieves its efficiency in the same way. This isn't to say that it cannot be the case. Second, Johansson and Larsson suggest that there is no superposition, interference, entanglement, contextuality, continuity of quantum state space, or quantum coherence in their QSL algorithms. Yet, the QSL model involves analogs of superposition, entanglement, and interference, and if there is an analog of superposition and interference, one would expect an analog of coherence as well.[49] So, the mere existence of an efficient QSL algorithm wouldn't seem to rule out quantum properties often appealed to to explain speedup. The same cannot be said of contextuality and continuity, which are both lacking in QSL models. Third, even if Johannsson and Larsson were right about additional information degrees of freedom being the source of quantum speedup, it would seem to be the case that in order for quantum systems to access and for us to make use of those degrees of freedom, one would require superposition, entanglement, coherence, and interference, rendering all of these features

---

[49] Physicists have recently been developing measures of coherence and thinking about how they apply to instances of quantum speedup. See Hillery (2016) to see how this applies in the context of the Deutsch–Jozsa algorithm.

explanatorily relevant. A careful analysis of QSL and associate algorithms would be required to establish to what extent multipartite entanglement and other quantum features are not responsible for quantum speedup.

6.7 Conclusions

Explaining quantum speedup is the central foundational challenge with respect to quantum computing. I hope to have made clear that there is no general easy answer. That said, I think it is useful to attempt a sketch of as general an explanation of quantum speedup as is feasible right now.

First, the degrees of freedom associated with the computational problem to be solved are efficiently matched (in space and energy) by degrees of freedom associated with the quantum system's linear evolution and ability to be in superposition states. This allows one to generate a state correlated to all values of a function efficiently, whereby we can extract partial information from that function efficiently. Unbounded multipartite entanglement is often required to generate this state as in Simon's algorithm and Shor's algorithm. Other times, as in Bernstein and Vazirani's algorithm, no entanglement is required to generate such a state. Second, problems have to be globally structured in some way, else *exponential* speedup appears out of reach. Third, there has to be an efficient way to extract such global information using interference to place the system in a subspace associated with the desired result.

Given the above facts, we can expect that there may be a good deal of variety to be found from algorithm to algorithm. We shouldn't expect exactly the same properties of quantum systems to explain speedup in every case. Study and comparison of algorithms should prove to be useful on a case-by-case basis. Newly devised measures of interference might help us classify different kinds of algorithms so that we can find important commonalities and differences. QSL and perhaps other toy models might prove useful in helping to sort what is essential in a quantum algorithm from what is ancillary for explaining quantum speedup. This will require very careful work.

Undoubtedly, the most important recent result in quantum computing is in Raz and Tal (2019). They prove that, relative to an oracle, **BQP** and **PH** separate. **PH** is a complexity class that contains **P**, **NP**, and **co-NP**, among others. See Dean (2016) for a definition of **PH**. Aaronson (2010) describes the quantum algorithms required. Previous results demonstrated separation only for subsets of **PH**. So, it is the most significant separation result to date. For one that is seeking to understand quantum speedup, an analysis of this result represents the state of the art, and maybe, just maybe, would reveal the secrets of quantum computing.

References

Aaronson, S. (2010). BQP and the polynomial hierarchy. In *Proceedings of the Forty-Second ACM Symposium on Theory of Computing* (pp. 141–150). New York: Association for Computing Machinery.

Aaronson, S. (2011). The equivalence of sampling and searching. In A. Kulikov & N. Vershchagin (eds.), *Lecture notes in computer science* (vol. 6651, pp. 1–14). Berlin, Heidelberg: Springer.

Aaronson, S., & Ambainis, A. (2014). The need for structure in quantum speedups. *Theory of Computing, 6*, 133–166.

Aharonov, D., van Dam, W., Kempe, J. et al. (2007). Adiabatic quantum computation is equivalent to standard quantum computation. *SIAM Journal on Computing, 37*(1), 166–194.

Albash, T., & Lidar, D. A. (2018, Jan). Adiabatic quantum computation. *Rev. Mod. Phys., 90*, 015002.

Ambainis, A. (2019). Understanding quantum algorithms via query complexity. In B. Sirakov, P. N. de Souza, & M. Viana (eds.), *Proceedings of the International Congress of Mathematicians (ICM2018)* (pp. 3265–3285). World Scientific.

Anderson, N. G. (2019). Information processing artifacts. *Minds and Machines, 29*, 193–225.

Andréka, H., Madarász, J. X., Németi, I., Németi, P., & Székely, G. (2018). Relativistic computation. In M. E. Cuffaro & S. C. Fletcher (eds.), *Physical perspectives on computation, computational perspectives on physics* (pp. 195–216). Cambridge University Press.

Annovi, F. (2015). Exploring quantum speed-up through cluster-state computers (unpublished doctoral dissertation). University of Bologna.

Beals, R., Buhrman, H., Cleve, R., Mosca, M., & de Wolf, R. (2001, July). Quantum lower bounds by polynomials. *Journal of the ACM, 48*(4), 778–797.

Bennett, C. H., Bernstein, E., Brassard, G., & Vazirani, U. (1997). Strengths and weaknesses of quantum computing. *SIAM Journal on Computing, 26*(5), 1510–1523.

Bennett, C. H., & DiVincenzo, D. P. (2000). Quantum information and computation. *Nature, 404*(6775), 247–255.

Bernstein, E., & Vazirani, U. (1997). Quantum complexity theory. *SIAM Journal on Computing, 26*(5), 1411–1473.

Braun, D., & Georgeot, B. (2006, Feb). Quantitative measure of interference. *Physical Review A, 73*, 022314.

Braun, D., & Georgeot, B. (2008, Feb). Interference versus success probability in quantum algorithms with imperfections. *Physical Review A, 77*, 022318.

Bub, J. (2010). Quantum computation: Where does the speed-up come from. In A. Bokulich & G. Jaegger (eds.), *Philosophy of quantum information and entanglement* (p. 231–246). Cambridge: Cambridge University Press.

Chalmers, D. J. (1996). Does a rock implement every finite-state automoton. *Synthese, 108*, 309–333.

Church, A. (1936). An unsolvable problem in elementary number theory. *American Journal of Mathematics, 58*(2), 345–363.

Church, A. (1937). Review of "A. M. Turing. On computable numbers, with an application to the Entscheidungsproblem." *Journal of Symbolic Logic, 2*(1), 42–43.

Cleve, R., Ekert, A., Macchiavello, C., & Mosca, M. (1998). Quantum algorithms revisited. *Proceedings of the Royal Society of London A, 454*, 339–354.

Copeland, B. (1996). What is computation? *Synthese, 108*(3), 335–359.

Copeland, B. (2002). Hypercomputation. *Minds and Machines, 12*(4), 461–502.

Copeland, B. (2004). Computable numbers: A guide. In B. Copeland (ed.), *The essential Turing: Seminal writings in computing, logic, philosophy, artificial intelligence, and artificial life.* Oxford: Oxford University Press.

Copeland, B. (2019). The Church-Turing thesis. In E. N. Zalta (ed.), *The Stanford encyclopedia of philosophy* (Spring 2019 ed.). Metaphysics Research Lab, Stanford University. https://plato.stanford.edu/archives/spr2019/entries/church-turing/.

Copeland, B., & Shagrir, O. (2007). Physical computation: How general are Gandy's principles for mechanisms? *Minds and Machines, 17*, 217–231.

Copeland, B., Shagrir, O., & Sprevak, M. (2018). Zeus's thesis, Gandy's thesis, and Penrose's thesis. In M. E. Cuffaro & S. Fletcher (eds.), *Physical perspectives on computation, computational perspectives on physics.* Cambridge: Cambridge University Press.

Cuffaro, M. E. (2012). Many worlds, the cluster-state quantum computer, and the problem of the preferred basis. *Studies in History and Philosophy of Modern Physics, 43*, 35–42.

Cuffaro, M. E. (2013). On the physical explanation for quantum speedup (unpublished doctoral dissertation). The University of Western Ontario, London, Ontario.

Cuffaro, M. E. (2015). How-possibly explanations in (quantum) computer science. *Philosophy of Science, 82*(5), 737–748.

Cuffaro, M. E. (2017). On the significance of the Gottesman–Knill theorem. *The British Journal for the Philosophy of Science, 68*(1), 91–121.

Cuffaro, M. E. (2018). Universality, invariance, and the foundations of computational complexity in the light of the quantum computer. In S. Hansson (ed.), *Technology and mathematics: Philosophical and historical investigations* (pp. 253–282). Springer.

Cuffaro, M. E. (in press). The philosophy of quantum computing. In E. R. Miranda (ed.), *Quantum computing in the arts and humanities.* Cham: Springer Nature.

Datta, A., Flammia, S. T., & Caves, C. M. (2005, Oct). Entanglement and the power of one qubit. *Physical Review A, 72*, 042316.

Davies, M. (2013). Three proofs of the undecidability of the Entscheidungsproblem. In S. B. Cooper & J. v. Leeuwen (eds.), *Alan Turing: His work and impact* (p. 49–52). San Diego: Elsevier Science.

Dean, W. (2016). Computational complexity theory. In E. N. Zalta (ed.), *The Stanford encyclopedia of philosophy* (Winter 2016 ed.). Metaphysics Research Lab, Stanford University. https://plato.stanford.edu/archives/win2016/entries/computational-complexity/.

Del Mol, L. (2019). Turing machines. In E. N. Zalta (ed.), *The Stanford encyclopedia of philosophy* (Winter 2019 ed.). Metaphysics Research Lab, Stanford University. https://plato.stanford.edu/archives/win2019/entries/turing-machine/

Deutsch, D. (1985). Quantum theory, the Church–Turing principle and the universal quantum computer. *Proceedings of the Royal Society of London A, 400*, 97–117.

Deutsch, D., & Jozsa, R. (1992). Rapid solutions of problems by quantum computation. *Proceedings of the Royal Society of London A, 439*, 553–558.

Dewhurst, J. (2018). Computing mechanisms without proper functions. *Minds and Machines, 28*, 569–588.

Duwell, A. (2007). The many-worlds interpretation and quantum computation. *Philosophy of Science, 74*(5), 1007–1018.

Duwell, A. (2017). Exploring the frontiers of computation: Measurement based quantum computers and the mechanistic view of computation. In A. Bokulich & J. Floyd (eds.), *Turing 100: Philosophical explorations of the legacy of Alan Turing* (vol. 324, pp. 219–232). Cham: Springer.

Duwell, A. (2018). How to make orthogonal positions parallel: Revisiting the quantum parallelism thesis. In M. E. Cuffaro & S. Fletcher (eds.), *Physical perspectives on computation, computational perspectives on physics.* Cambridge: Cambridge University Press.

Earman, J. (1986). *A primer on determinism.* D. Reidel Pub. Co.

Earman, J., & Norton, J. (1993, March). Forever is a day – supertasks in Pitowski and Malament-Hogarth spacetimes. *Philosophy of Science, 60*(1), 22–42.

Ekert, A., & Jozsa, R. (1998). Quantum algorithms: entanglement-enhanced information processing. *Philosophical Transactions of the Royal Society of London A, 356,* 1769–1782.

Feynman, R. P. (1982). Simulating physics with computers. *International Journal of Theoretical Physics, 21*(6), 467–488.

Feynman, R. P. (1985, Feb). Quantum mechanical computers. *Optics News, 11*(2), 11–20.

Fletcher, S. C. (2018). Computers in abstraction/representation theory. *Minds and Machines, 28*(3), 445–463.

Fortnow, L. (2003). One complexity theorist's view of quantum computing. *Theoretical Computer Science, 292,* 597–610.

Freedman, M. H., Kitaev, A., & Larson, M. J. (2003). Topological quantum computation. *Bulletin of the American Mathematical Society, 40,* 31–38.

Fresco, N. (2013). *Physical computation and cognitive science.* New York: Springer.

Frigg, R., & Nguyen, J. (2020). Scientific representation. In E. N. Zalta (ed.), *The Stanford encyclopedia of philosophy* (Spring 2020 ed.). Metaphysics Research Lab, Stanford University. https://plato.stanford.edu/archives/spr2020/entries/scientific-representation/.

Gandy, R. (1980). Church's thesis and principles for mechanisms. In J. Barwise, H. J. Keisler, & K. Kunen (eds.), *The Kleene symposium* (vol. 101, pp. 123–148). Elsevier.

Godfrey-Smith, P. (2009, Aug 01). Triviality arguments against functionalism. *Philosophical Studies, 145*(2), 273–295.

Gross, D., Flammia, S. T., & Eisert, J. (2009, May). Most quantum states are too entangled to be useful as computational resources. *Physical Review Letters, 102,* 190501.

Grzegorczyk, A. (1957). On the definitions of computable real continuous functions. *Fundamenta Mathematicae, 44*(1), 61–71.

Hagar, A., & Cuffaro, M. (2019). Quantum computing. In E. N. Zalta (ed.), *The Stanford encyclopedia of philosophy* (Winter 2019 ed.). Metaphysics Research Lab, Stanford University. https://plato.stanford.edu/archives/win2019/entries/qt-quantcomp/.

Harris, R., Lanting, T., Berkley, A. et al. (2009, Aug). Compound Josephson-junction coupler for flux qubits with minimal crosstalk. *Physical Review B, 80,* 052506.

Hewitt-Horsman, C. (2009). An introduction to many worlds in quantum computation. *Foundations of Physics, 39*(8), 869–902.

Hilbert, D., & Ackermann, W. (1928). *Grundzüge der theoretischen Logik.* Berlin: Springer.

Hillery, M. (2016, Jan). Coherence as a resource in decision problems: The Deutsch–Jozsa algorithm and a variation. *Physical Review A, 93,* 012111.

Hogarth, M. L. (1992). Does general relativity allow an observer to view an eternity in a finite time? *Foundations of Physics Letters, 5*(2), 173–181. doi: https://doi.org/10.1007/BF00682813

Horsman, C., Kendon, V., & Stepney, S. (2017). The natural science of computing. *Communications of the ACM, 60*(8), 31–34.

Horsman, C., Kendon, V., Stepney, S., & Young, J. P. W. (2017). Abstraction and representation in living organisms: When does a biological system compute? In G. Dodig-Crnkovic & R. Giovangnoli (eds.), *Representation and reality in humans, other living organisms, and intelligent machines* (pp. 91–116). Cham: Springer International Publishing.

Horsman, C., Stepney, S., Wagner, R. C., & Kendon, V. (2014). When does a physical system compute? *Proceedings of the Royal Society of London A, 470,* 20140182.

Horsman, D. (2017). The representation of computation in physical systems. In M. Massimi, J. W. Romeijn, & G. Schurz (eds.), *EPSA15 selected papers* (pp. 191–204). Cham: Springer.

Horsman, D., Kendon, B., & Stepney, S. (2018). Abstraction/representation theory and the natural science of computation. In M. E. Cuffaro & S. C. Fletcher (eds.), *Physical perspectives on computation* (pp. 127–149). Cambridge: Cambridge University Press.

Horsman, D. C. (2015). Abstraction/representation theory for heterotic physical computing. *Philosophical Transactions of the Royal Society of London A, 373,* 20140224.

Johansson, N., & Larsson, J.Å. (2017). Efficient classical simulation of the Deutsch–Jozsa and Simon's algorithms. *Quantum Information Processing, 16*(9), 233.

Johansson, N., & Larsson, J.Å. (2019). Quantum simulation logic, oracles, and the quantum advantage. *Entropy, 21,* 800.

Josza, R., & Linden, N. (2003). On the role of entanglement on quantum-computational speed-up. *Proceedings of the Royal Society of London A, 459,* 2011–2032.

Kalai, G. (2020). The argument against quantum computers. In M. Hemmo & O. Shenker (eds.), *Quantum, probability, logic: The work and influence of Itamar Pitowsky* (pp. 399–422). Cham: Springer International Publishing.

Kato, T. (1950). On the adiabatic theorem of quantum mechanics. *Journal of the Physical Society of Japan, 5*(6), 435–439.

Kendon, V., Sebald, A., & Stepney, S. (2015). Heterotic computing: past, present, and future. *Philosophical Transactions of the Royal Society of London A, 373*, 20140225.

Kleene, S. (1953). *Introduction to metamathematics.* Amsterdam: North Holland.

Kleene, S. (1967). *Mathematical logic.* New York: Wiley.

Kripke, S. A. (2013). The Church-Turing "thesis" as a special corollary of Gödel's completeness theorem. In B. Copeland, C. Posy, & O. Shagrir (eds.), *Computability: Turing, Gödel, Church, and beyond* (p. 77–104). Cambridge, MA: Massachusetts Institute of Technology Press.

Ladyman, J. (2009). What does it mean to say that a physical system implements a computation? *Theoretical Computer Science, 410*, 376–383.

Lahtinen, V., & Pachos, J. K. (2017). A short introduction to topological quantum computation. *SciPost Phys., 3*, 021.

Lloyd, S. (1999, Dec). Quantum search without entanglement. *Physical Review B, 61*, 010301.

Longino, H. E. (1990). *Science as social knowledge: Values and objectivity in scientific inquiry.* Princeton: Princeton University Press.

Machamer, P., Darden, L., & Craver, C. F. (2000). Thinking about mechanisms. *Philosophy of Science, 67*(1), 1–25.

Maroney, O. (2009). Information processing and thermodynamic entropy. In E. N. Zalta (ed.), *The Stanford encyclopedia of philosophy* (Fall 2009 ed.). Metaphysics Research Lab, Stanford University. https://plato .stanford.edu/archives/fall2009/entries/information-entropy/.

Maroney, O. J. E., & Timpson, C. G. (2018). How is there a physics of information? On characterizing physical evolution as information processing. In M. E. Cuffaro & S. C. Fletcher (eds.), *Physical perspectives on computation, computational perspectives on physics* (pp. 103–126). Cambridge University Press.

Marr, D. (1982). *Vision.* San Francisco: W. H. Freeman.

Meyer, D. A. (2000, Aug). Sophisticated quantum search without entanglement. *Physical Review Letters, 85*, 2014–2017.

Milkowski, M. (2013). *Explaining the computational mind.* Cambridge, MA: Massachusetts Institute of Technology Press.

Neilsen, M., & Chuang, I. (2000). *Quantum computation and quantum infomation.* Cambridge: Cambridge University Press.

Piccinini, G. (2007). Computing mechanisms. *Philosophy of Science, 74*(4), 501–526.

Piccinini, G. (2008). Computation without representation. *Philosophical Studies, 137*(2), 205–241.

Piccinini, G. (2015). *Physical computation: A mechanistic account.* Oxford: Oxford University Press.

Piccinini, G., & Bahar, S. (2013). Neural computation and the computational theory of cognition. *Cognitive Science, 34*, 453–488.

Pitowsky, I. (1990). The physical Church thesis and physical computational complexity. *Iyyun, 39*, 81–99.

Pitowsky, I. (2002). Quantum speed-up of computations. *Philosophy of Science, 69*(3), S168–S177.

Pitowsky, I. (2007). From logic to physics: How the meaning of computation changed over time. In S. B. Cooper, B. Löwe, & A. Sorbi (eds.), *Computation and logic in the real world* (pp. 621–631). Berlin, Heidelberg: Springer Berlin Heidelberg.

Pour-El, M. B., & Richards, I. (1981). The wave equation with computable initial data such that its unique solution is not computable. *Advances in Mathematics, 39*(3), 215–239.

Putnam, H. (1988). *Representation and reality.* Cambridge, MA: Massachusetts Institute of Technology Press.

Raussendorf, R., & Briegel, H. (2001). A one-way quantum computer. *Physical Review Letters, 86*(5188).

Raz, R., & Tal, A. (2019). Oracle separation of BQP and PH. In *Proceedings of the 51st annual ACM SIGACT symposium on theory of computing* (pp. 13–23). New York: Association for Computing Machinery.

Rescorla, M. (2014). A theory of computational implementation. *Synthese, 191*, 1277–1307.

Roland, J., & Cerf, N. J. (2002, Mar). Quantum search by local adiabatic evolution. *Physical Review A, 65*, 042308.

Scheutz, M. (1999). When physical systems realize functions *Mind and Machines, 9*, 161–196.

Schweizer, P. (2019). Computation in physical systems: A normative mapping account. In D. Berkich & M. d'Alfonso (eds.), *On the cognitive, ethical, and scientific dimensions of artificial intelligence* (vol. 134, pp. 27–47). Cham: Springer.

Searle, J. R. (1992). *The rediscovery of the mind.* Cambridge, MA: Massachusetts Institute of Technology Press.

Shagrir, O. (2001). Content, computation, and externalism. *Mind, 110*(438), 369–400.

Shinbrot, T., Grebogi, C., Wisdom, J., & Yorke, J. A. (1992). Chaos in a double pendulum. *American Journal of Physics, 60*(6), 491–499.

Shor, P. W. (1994). Algorithms for quantum computation: discrete logarithms and factoring. In *Proceedings 35th Annual Symposium on Foundations of Computer Science* (pp. 124–134).

Sieg, W. (1994). Mechanical procedures and mathematical experience. In A. George (ed.), *Mathematics and mind* (pp. 71–117). Oxford University Press.

Sieg, W. (2002a). Calculations by man and machine: conceptual analysis. In W. Sieg, R. Sommer, & C. Tallcot (eds.), *Reflections on the foundations of mathematics: Essays in honor of Solomon Feferman* (pp. 390–409). CRC Press.

Sieg, W. (2002b). Calculations by man and machine: mathematical presentation. In P. Gärdenfors, J. Woleñski, & K. Kajania-Placek (eds.), *In the scope of logic, methodology, and philosophy of science* (vol. 1, pp. 247–262). Netherlands: Kluwer Academic Publishers.

Spekkens, R. W. (2007). Evidence for the epistemic view of states. *Physical Review A, 75*, 032110.

Sprevak, M. (2018). Triviality arguments about computational implementation. In M. Sprevak & M. Colombo (eds.), *Routledge handbook of the computational mind* (pp. 175–191). London: Routledge.

Stahlke, D. (2014, Aug). Quantum interference as a resource for quantum speedup. *Physical Review A, 90*, 022302.

Steane, A. (2003). A quantum computer needs only one universe. *Studies in History and Philosophy of Modern Physics, 34*, 469–478.

Timpson, C. G. (2013). *Quantum information theory and the foundations of quantum mechanics.* Oxford: Oxford University Press.

Timpson, C. G., & Brown, H. R. (2005). Proper and improper separability. *International Journal of Quantum Information, 3*(4), 679–690.

Turing, A. (1936). On computable numbers, with an application to the Entscheidungsproblem. *Proceedings of the London Mathematical Society, 42*(1), 230–265.

Turing, A. (1937). Computability and λ-definability. *The Journal of Symbolic Logic, 2*(4), 153–163.

van Fraassen, B. C. (2006). Representation: The problem for structuralism. *Philosophy of Science, 73*(5), 536–547.

Vollmer, H. (1999). Introduction to Circuit Complexity: A Uniform Approach. Italy: Springer-Verlag.

Wallace, D. (2012). *The emergent multiverse: Quantum theory according to the Everett interpretation.* Oxford: Oxford University Press.

Yoran, N., & Short, A. J. (2007, Oct). Efficient classical simulation of the approximate quantum Fourier transform. *Physical Review A, 76*, 042321.

Acknowledgments

Though shorter than some, this is my first lengthy publication, and I want to recognize some people who helped me get to this point. Two people stand above others: Nancy Nersessian, my undergraduate mentor, and John Norton, my thesis advisor. Both of them were very patient with me, very generous with their time, and helped me immeasurably. I have had many discussions over the years about computation with many people, and the following individuals have been especially helpful: Neal Anderson, Jeff Bub, Mike Cuffaro, John Earman, Sam Fletcher, Amit Hagar, Wayne Myrvold, John Norton, Gualtiero Piccinini, Itamar Pitowsky, and Chris Timpson. A very special thank-you goes out to Mike Cuffaro, Sam Fletcher, Soazig Le Bihan, Gualtiero Piccinini, and two anonymous referees who were kind enough to give me feedback. Breaking with tradition, I blame them for any errors in this Element. I jest. I also thank James Owen Weatherall, who edits the Elements in the Philosophy of Physics series, for affording me the opportunity to write this Element. Finally, this Element would have been impossible to write were it not for the support of my wife and two children.

This Element is dedicated to Jon Johnston and Rob Clifton, two philosophers, both incredible in very different ways, who are no longer with us, and who played very important roles in my life.

The Philosophy of Physics

James Owen Weatherall

University of California, Irvine

James Owen Weatherall is Professor of Logic and Philosophy of Science at the University of California, Irvine. He is the author, with Cailin O'Connor, of *The Misinformation Age: How False Beliefs Spread* (Yale, 2019), which was selected as a *New York Times Editors'* Choice and Recommended Reading by *Scientific American*. His previous books were *Void: The Strange Physics of Nothing* (Yale, 2016) and the *New York Times* bestseller *The Physics of Wall Street: A Brief History of Predicting the Unpredictable* (Houghton Mifflin Harcourt, 2013). He has published approximately fifty peer-reviewed research articles in leading physics and philosophy of science journals and has delivered over 100 invited academic talks and public lectures.

About the Series

This Cambridge Elements series provides concise and structured introductions to all the central topics in the philosophy of physics. The Elements in the series are written by distinguished senior scholars and bright junior scholars with relevant expertise, producing balanced, comprehensive coverage of multiple perspectives in the philosophy of physics.

Cambridge Elements ☰

The Philosophy of Physics

CPSIA information can be obtained
at www.ICGtesting.com
Printed in the USA
LVHW081644180921
698160LV00013B/339

9 781009 108553